D1526322

Sweden: A Modern Democracy
on Ancient Foundations

SWEDEN

A Modern Democracy on Ancient Foundations

NILS HERLITZ

Professor of Public Law in the
University of Stockholm

The University of Minnesota Press, Minneapolis

LONDON · HUMPHREY MILFORD · OXFORD UNIVERSITY PRESS

FOREWORD

THE author of this concise and informative work on Swedish government, politics, and constitutional development visited the United States in 1938 to participate in the celebration of the tercentenary of the Swedish settlements on the Delaware. Previously known in America only by a relatively few scholars he won the friendship and respect of hundreds who met him and heard him speak, formally and informally, on his tour across the country.

Born August 7, 1888, Professor Herlitz entered the University of Uppsala in 1906. While obtaining there a liberal education he concentrated particularly in history, and became a protégé of the well-known Professor Harold Hjärne. Ten years after entering the university Professor Herlitz became a Doctor of Philosophy and also docent or instructor in history at Uppsala. In the following years he served not only as a university teacher but also for several years as secretary to the constitution committee of the *riksdag*, and, from 1919 to 1927, as leader of the *Stadshistoriska Institutet* (Institute of Municipal History). In the latter capacity he published in 1927 a collection of all the medieval privileges of the older Swedish cities. These contacts with the constitutional problems of both national and local governments, and with the practical problems of governmental administration, turned his attention more and more to constitutional and administrative law.

In 1920 he transferred from the University of Uppsala to the University of Stockholm. He was advanced to assistant professor of administrative law in 1925, and to professor of public law (constitutional, administrative, and international law) in 1927. This work also entailed the teaching of political science until 1935, but in recent years he has given his attention almost entirely to legal studies, and particularly to administrative law. In 1936 the University of Stockholm made him Doctor of Law *honoris causa,* and in 1938 he became editor of *Förvaltningsrättslig Tidskrift* (Administrative Law Review).

Many other activities of public importance to Sweden and to the northern countries have also drawn upon his energies and benefited from his counsel. In the highly successful efforts to draw the northern countries into closer cooperation he has performed numerous services, including the editing of *Nordisk Tidskrift* since 1922, assisting in the revision of history textbooks to promote better understanding, initiating a Nordic meeting in 1930 for the study of constitutional law and political science, and serving as secretary and board member of the Swedish branch of the society *Norden.* Since 1934 he has been a member of the county council of the Stockholm district. He is chairman of the Swedish National Defense League, and he recently became a Senator, that is to say, a member of the upper house of the Swedish *riksdag.*

These numerous public services, while giving him a deep insight into the government and problems of his country and keeping his studies and his teaching close to the realities of politics, have not prevented him from doing a prodigious amount of scholarly work. His publications comprise scholarly monographs in the field of history; treatises on administrative law, constitutional law, and constitutional history; expert reports on municipal courts and on the publication of government documents; textbooks on government and constitutional history for the schools; several popular works on Swedish government; and a collection of essays on self-government. To know the government and the public law of Sweden one cannot neglect the reading of a number of his books.

To the English-reading public he now offers this comprehensive yet succinct survey of Swedish government and the essentials of its historical background. This work he wrote in English; the undersigned left the exposition very much as he wrote it, but made some changes here and there to make the text more understandable to American readers. On the whole we feel that he has achieved excellence—to have presented in so brief a work not only the essential facts of Swedish government but also so much of the spirit and the life of the Swedish people and their politics.

WILLIAM ANDERSON
GEORGE M. STEPHENSON

University of Minnesota
March, 1939

PREFACE

In connection with the celebration of the tercentenary of the first Swedish settlement in America the author was invited by several universities in the United States to lecture, in April and May, 1938, on the following topics: Constitutional Government in Sweden Three Hundred Years Ago and Today, Public Administration and Civil Service in Sweden, and Government and Citizen in Sweden. The present publication is based on these lectures, which have, however, been amplified and rearranged.

Many people have come to regard Sweden as a well organized and happy democracy and to take interest in its social, economic, and political conditions. This interest has perhaps centered in the social and economic developments there. In my lectures, however, I confined myself, as I do in this book, to the legal and constitutional foundations of Swedish life. Such references as I have made to social and economic conditions, of which I make no claim to expert knowledge, are only incidental.

I may, however, be allowed to emphasize that those aspects of Swedish life which I treat, though very little understood in foreign countries, should be taken into account by anyone who aspires to know the Sweden of today. To gain an idea of its life one must not neglect its political institutions, for they have influenced its social and economic conditions in a decisive way; and to explain the political institutions of today it was necessary to pay some attention to their historical growth during the centuries. Just as in England so in Sweden political and constitutional institutions are built on foundations laid in remote times. They cannot be properly understood unless the background is kept in mind.

As a matter of fact, the historical development of the Swedish constitution may be studied with profit also by those who are interested rather in the general aspects of government than in the particular institutions of Sweden. Swedish history has indeed a character of its own. The country has retained throughout the centuries, from primitive times, some elements of popular government and political freedom. What the European peoples learned in the nineteenth century from the American and French revolutions, and from constitutional government in England, was not altogether new to Sweden, which affords the rare spectacle of a modern democracy with direct roots in the Middle Ages. Its constitutional history is comparable to that of England, but other countries offer no clear parallels. The other Scandinavian countries, Denmark and Norway, have gone quite another way, passing through that stage of monarchic absolutism well known from general European history. Therefore the constitutional history of Sweden may claim a certain amount of attention not only for its own sake but also as an indigenous and original contribution to the practical experiences of popular government and political freedom.

In writing on Swedish political institutions for American readers, many of whom may look to my country for guidance in the difficult social problems of today, I feel obliged to make some qualifying remarks. When I was young many people in my country regarded the United States as something of a wonderland, where most of the social and political problems had been solved under the aegis of democracy, whereas Sweden seemed to be hopelessly behind in its development. The stream of emigrants going to the West confirmed, to that generation, the notion that there was something fundamentally wrong with the old country. This view was perhaps somewhat exaggerated. I am quite sure however that nowadays, on the other hand, many people overemphasize the value of Swedish performances in economic and social politics, in government and administration. As a Swedish citizen I know very well that in my country many things are not as they should be, and I have no desire to spread the idea that Sweden is a democratic utopia. It may be, however, that I shall not be able to make our faults, our difficulties, and our unsolved problems sufficiently clear. In attempting to give a short survey of the political institutions of a country and to explain them as a whole, as founded on the history of its people and as expressing its spirit, one can scarcely avoid laying more stress on the rationality of the institutions than on criticism and discussion. I must therefore ask the reader who may be struck by the lights of the picture always to remember that there are shadows too.

This is not meant to be a textbook of exact and exhaustive factual knowledge. I have felt I must instead try to grasp and emphasize those particular features that give the institutions of my country their spirit, their proper character. I realize that a more profound knowledge of American institutions might have enabled me to see more distinctly all the differences and points of similarity that would make the picture of Sweden clear to American readers. Undoubtedly I incur the risk of including things of which American readers will say "Well, that seems to be just like this country and a good many other countries too."

On the other hand I may fail to emphasize, or even mention, facts that are important but that I am inclined to take for granted.

Some of these difficulties have, however, been overcome during my lecturing trip. On my visits to American universities I have had the advantage of meeting a great many professors and students interested in constitutional and administrative law, government, and public administration, and to discuss with them matters of common interest. These discussions, and the questions put to me after my lectures, have helped me greatly to understand both American institutions and the points of view from which Americans are likely to see the corresponding institutions of my country. For these frequent exchanges of information and ideas and the broader knowledge resulting from them I am profoundly grateful. They are for me among the most valuable results of my visit to the United States, and have been distinctly helpful to me in revising my lectures for publication.

I wish to express my thanks to the University of Minnesota Press for publishing this book. I should be particularly pleased if it enables some of the many students and graduates of the University of Minnesota who are of Swedish descent to know the country from which their forefathers came. It seems to me that if American scholars of Swedish descent come to take an increasing interest in Swedish institutions they may help answer a question of no little importance for both countries, a question I could not escape asking again and again when I came in contact with Swedish Americans: Have the Swedes who came to America, especially those who formed distinctively Swedish communities, large or small, brought with them anything from their old country—political or social forms, habits, or traditions? Has the political behavior that had developed in Sweden before their migration thereby influenced American life? I feel that my book will not be useless if it furthers or stimulates the study of such problems.

I am very much indebted to my friends Professor William Anderson and Professor George Stephenson of the University of Minnesota, who kindly undertook the heavy task of correcting my manuscript, particularly in respect to language.

NILS HERLITZ

Harvard University
June, 1938

CONTENTS

Sweden: A Modern Democracy
on Ancient Foundations

A CONSTITUTIONAL STATE

SWEDEN has a constitutional government. This government, however, was not an invention of the nineteenth century. It has, on the contrary, very old traditions. One may question how far it is right to use such a term as constitutional government for an age when conditions were quite different from those of modern times, but this problem will not be gone into here. It may be enough to trace briefly some of the threads connecting the Middle Ages with our constitutional government of today.

Constitutional government presupposes a rule of law regulating not only the relations among citizens but also the working of public authority and its relation to citizens. Now the old idea of the supremacy of law has always had a strong foothold in Swedish life, and the rule of law has meant the rule of written law. It is a salient feature of Swedish legal history that we have never been content with judge-made law. There has been a constant tendency to make the law familiar to everybody—from early medieval times when the laws were periodically recited to the communities in their regular meetings (*things*), through the great codifications of the fourteenth and eighteenth centuries, down to modern statute-making. And there has never been any doubt that the laws should be binding upon the king and his servants as well as upon the citizens.

For a long time it has also been felt that the scope of public authority particularly should be regulated by law. A special part of the land law of the fourteenth century was devoted to this subject. There the duties of the king and people were described in the form of oaths to be delivered by both parties when a king ascended the throne. The oath of the king prevented him, for instance, from doing such things as giving new laws and imposing new taxes without the consent of the people. Down to the end of the seventeenth century, if not later, these rules remained in force.

The duties of the king and the limits of his authority were also described, more comprehensively, in the charters he had to give at his accession to the throne. Such charters are typical of the elective kingdoms of the Middle Ages. When, in other countries, the elective monarchies were transformed to hereditary ones, the monarchs were generally freed from the obligation of buying the crown by such concessions, but in Sweden the kingdom did not become hereditary before the middle of the sixteenth century. Even after that time several circumstances made the accession of the kings dependent on the good will of the people. Gustavus Adolphus, for instance, could not have gained the crown in 1611 if he had not bound himself by a charter. The resemblance of this charter to a modern constitution is striking; it is one of the apparent links between Magna Charta and modern constitutionalism.

One more step in the same direction was taken after the death of Gustavus Adolphus in 1632. The charter lost its force when the king died, but in 1634 there was promulgated a law concerning the government which was meant to remain in force independently of changes on the throne. It was called the "form of government" (*regeringsform*), a term we still use for our principal constitutional law. Perhaps it could also be translated, in the terminology of Cromwell nineteen years later, "instrument of government." Although it is true that this document differed in content from a modern constitution—it had more to say about the organization of the government than about the rights of the people and the prerogatives of parliament— in many respects it may be regarded as a predecessor of modern constitutionalism. We are often told that the history of written constitutions begins with Cromwell and the American colonies, but the Swedish regeringsform of 1634 ought not to be forgotten.

To be sure, there was later, from 1680 to 1718, a short period when the king reigned absolutely, or almost so; but in 1719 the constitutional idea was revived by a new charter and a new "form of government." The scope of these documents, taken together, quite corresponds to that of a modern constitution. And since that time political life in Sweden has always been regulated by special constitutional laws, distinct from other laws and statutes. We had, until 1772, the royal charters, given at the king's accession to the throne; and we have had the regeringsformer of 1720, 1772, and 1809, the latter being still in force.*

In the content of these constitutional laws many changes may be observed. The regeringsformer have, for instance, ceased to regulate, as did that of 1634, the administrative organization of the realm; instead, the later constitutional laws have much to say about the organization of the parliament (*riksdag*) and its relation to the king. But the connection between the successive constitutional laws is evident. An analysis of the various sections of the regerings-

---

*Besides the regeringsform, the principal constitutional law, there are today other laws that are regarded as constitutional (*grundlagar*) : one concerning the organization of the parliament (*riksdagsordning*), one concerning the succession to the throne (*successionsordning*), and one concerning the liberty of the press (*tryckfrihetsförordning*).

form now in force reveals pretty clearly that parts of earlier regeringsformer and royal charters have been their prototypes. Many formulations date from the seventeenth and eighteenth centuries, and one remarkable section derives from the medieval land law.

In studying modern constitutions it is customary to distinguish the stipulations concerning the rights of citizens from those organizing the state and distributing the powers between different authorities. Now in earlier times the main task of those laws and statutes that I have described as more or less constitutional was to prevent the king from infringing arbitrarily upon the freedom of the citizens. This is true even of the regulations limiting the king's rights in such things as taxation and legislation, for these were thought of as safeguarding the individual rights of citizens. As a matter of fact they did not confer any powers on particular bodies by which the popular will was to be represented. Neither the land law nor the early charters stated in what form, or through what organs, the consent of the people should be given. This is typical of the medieval point of view.

Gradually, however, the riksdag came to exercise those powers which belonged, in principle, to the citizens; the voice of the people was heard in its decisions. Swedish law was not far removed from the well-known English doctrine that every Englishman is present in parliament. Thus it is quite natural that little attention should be paid to safeguarding the individual rights of the citizens against the riksdag.

Since the eighteenth century, therefore, Sweden's constitutional laws have been mainly concerned with the organization of the executive and legislative powers and with their mutual relations; in these laws there is still no counterpart to the declarations of rights found in most other constitutions. The only section that may be compared with them is one that contains a sort of translation from the old land law of the fourteenth century and describes in archaic words the duty of the king to maintain law and private rights. It did not occur to the constitutional fathers of 1809 that the riksdag would not be an adequate guardian for the rights of the citizens. They believed in the thesis of Montesquieu, that a balance of powers will secure individual liberty. Founded as it is on historical traditions the Swedish constitution has been little affected by that great movement which aimed at defining and securing a sphere of freedom for the individual. This does not mean that our constitutional traditions were hostile or indifferent to individual liberty—far from that. We boast of having always been a free people, and not without right. A certain amount of freedom has always been looked upon as the indispensable foundation of a sound society, but in Sweden it has been left to the law, made with the consent of the people, to define the content of this freedom. Thus, just as in England, the backbone of the liberty of the citizens has always consisted in their ability to act, to take part in public affairs. Their liberty has followed from their political influence.

Consequently, in later times, the position of the citizens has shifted according to the actual opinions prevailing in the riksdag and to the exigencies of the times. No rigid constitution has fettered the development of legislation. And if the courts have the power to invalidate a statute as being unconstitutional—it is not easy to say whether they do have that power or not—this does not mean, at any rate, that they can safeguard the rights of the citizens against new claims from the state, since the constitution has nothing to say about them. The modern ideas of state activity and state socialism have poured in without meeting constitutional difficulties. Naturally there has been a good deal of struggle over how far the state should go in attacking freedom and property, but the question has always been merely political, not constitutional. Only recently, however, the question has been raised whether the time has not come, now that a monistic form of government seems to have been substituted for a dualistic one, to inscribe in our constitution some principles concerning the rights and the liberty of the citizens.

There is also another difference between the Swedish and the American conceptions of constitutional government. In earlier times, certainly, the constitutional laws were intended to regulate the exercise of public authority in a very permanent way. The regeringsform of 1634, for instance, was intended to be "everlasting." Here the influence of political thought may be observed. Learned men and politicians used to look at constitutional laws from the point of view of contemporary doctrines; accordingly they learned as early as the seventeenth century to regard them as "fundamental laws"—a term which is still used (*grundlag*)—and in the eyes of the eighteenth century they were in a way the codification of the so-called social contract. But this idea of a very rigid constitution has not been maintained; the constitutional laws are very flexible. They may be altered by a simple majority vote of both chambers, repeated after new elections to the Second Chamber. As a matter of fact they have been amended very often. In the principal constitutional law, the regeringsform, very few sections remain as they were in 1809. Political life and the development of society are allowed to proceed without too much regard for principles once embodied in the constitution. Furthermore, considerable changes have taken place in the structure of our government without corresponding changes in the constitutional laws.

American students may thus, for several reasons, be inclined to think that the constitutional principle is not very important in Sweden. I still think it is. There are of course instances where constitutional regulations have not been strictly observed by the political powers; our history records many aggressions of the king and of the riksdag. Even in modern times cases can be found where constitutional rules have not been duly considered. But although there have sometimes been constitutional developments *contra legem,* on the whole it may be said that the constitutional principle is earnestly sustained. The men active in government and riksdag do not usually forget the fundamental principle that they, as well as private citizens, are acting under a rule of law. The constitutionality of various acts of government is a constant topic of public discussion, and I think it is no exaggeration to say that government and riksdag are observing the rules that bind them nearly as well as if they were subject to the control of law courts. Thus the Swedish government may really, though not in the same sense as the government of the United States, be described as a government of laws, not of men, a constitutional government.

9

CONSTITUTIONAL GOVERNMENT
THREE HUNDRED YEARS AGO

THE Swedish constitutional government of three hundred years ago is the one that the people who settled in Delaware in 1638 grew up under; beginning the discussion there thus seems fitting, for it may reveal some political and social traditions brought to America from over the sea. American students of political and constitutional history take a great interest in analyzing their inheritance from English life in the beginning of the seventeenth century, and the contribution of the English settlers is well known. It may also be of some interest to know a little about that far-off country from which the men of 1638 came, since it is possible that their ideas and traditions have survived and affected, in some little way, the development of American life and American institutions. But the truth is that nothing is known of such an influence, and there are reasons for doubting that there was any. Even aside from the small number of early Swedish emigrants as compared with English, there was an enormous difference between them: the men from old England came to America anxious to realize the religious and political ideals with which they were imbued; the Swedes had no such aspirations.

There is, however, another reason why a short survey of Swedish constitutional history could conveniently start with the beginning of the seventeenth century. We are used to looking back to those times as something of a golden age. Such a notion ought, of course, to be judged critically. But as a matter of fact the first half of the seventeenth century, and especially the reign of Gustavus Adolphus (1611–32), was of a significance that can hardly be overemphasized in the development of Sweden, and in many fields men still feel the influence of those days.

Sweden had been a comparatively primitive agricultural community, somewhat remote from the great struggles of Europe and from the great streams of European culture. In the time of the Counter Reformation, however, there was a considerable change. The waves of Catholic expansion met a people in whom Protestant conviction had taken strong root. The Swedish people stood behind their princes in the fight for religious and political freedom just as the English did in Elizabeth's struggle with Spain. This situation finally, in 1630, led Sweden into the Thirty Years War, in which our armies had remarkable success under Gustavus Adolphus. As a consequence of these external difficulties, far-reaching changes in the structure of the Swedish community were brought about.

Students looking for confirmations of the well-known proposition that internal development is dependent upon the external situation should pay some attention to the history of Sweden in the days of Gustavus Adolphus and the decades after his death in 1632. There was a marvelous evolution in every department of social life—administration, communications, industry, trade, education. The great number of tercentenaries we are now celebrating remind us how many institutions that are still of great importance were founded in those remarkable times, when the typical national state, with its centralization, its control over production and trade, its standing army, and its finances, was molded into shape in a process of only a few decades.

Students of constitutional history also have good reason

for going back to those times. The constitutional development did not, of course, have its beginning with Gustavus Adolphus; but new forms of lasting importance were created; new habits and traditions were formed. A framework was built within which political life could develop for centuries. According to constitutional law the king had to collaborate in various ways with the people.

In the first place, several sorts of local communities and local institutions formed flourishing self-governments. The social evolution of the Middle Ages had not destroyed the ancient freedom of the farming class. In the rural assemblies known as hundred *things,* for example, the chief of the hundred with a board of farmers formed the court of first instance; in these *things* also several administrative questions of common interest were handled. Similarly, in parish meetings rectors met with parishioners for secular as well as ecclesiastical purposes. Rectors were, to a large extent, elected by their communities, a remarkably democratic feature of our constitution. The Catholic Church had not been able to change this system, although it was decidedly contrary to her principles. After the Reformation the rectors' position in the communities had strengthened. Particularly in the fight against the Catholic powers—a struggle at the same time religious and political—the clergy assumed a real leadership in both political and spiritual matters. During times of war in the seventeenth century municipal institutions grew increasingly important, since officers of the king often had to negotiate with their spokesmen when imposts, taxes, and conscriptions were to be levied. Behind the strenuous efforts of the Swedish people in the Thirty Years War lay countless laborious negotiations with free communities all over the realm.

Secondly, in the later Middle Ages the nobility had developed as a distinct group. In accordance with medieval traditions they were mainly a military class, with the duty of forming a knightly cavalry when the king called for their services. From ancient times they had had representation of a kind in the Council of the Realm (*riksråd*), which consisted of great landlords from different parts of the country. Sometimes all of the nobility were called to assemblies, or diets. On many occasions the nobility, and especially the council, had shown great independence, appearing as advocates of the rights of the people when they were thought to be menaced by the king.

In the days of Gustavus Adolphus, however, the nobility were finding new forms for their political activity. The military technique demanded a change; in Sweden as in other countries the medieval cavalry was being succeeded by troops raised in other ways. On the other hand, the nobility could render service in new forms. The new army needed officers; and above all, there was good use for their ability in the rapidly growing administrative work. As a matter of fact, the development of the state machinery raised a serious question. Should this machinery, this civil service, be built up from the old leading class, or should the work and the power connected with it be entrusted to people depending totally upon the king? For a time there had been a tendency to set the aristocracy aside. Some of the kings were jealous of their power, and many of the noblemen did not like laborious administrative work. But in the time of Gustavus Adolphus the king and the aristocracy shared a desire to make the old landed nobility with their military traditions the cornerstone of a new bureaucracy. Within a few decades they were in fact thus transformed.

This transformation had, however, certain constitutional consequences. When the aristocracy entered the royal service it was not in order to become dependent, blind tools of the monarch. They were granted an independent status, with security against such things as arbitrary removal; and the functions of the different administrative authorities and their relations to the king were carefully described, especially in the regeringsform of 1634. This may be called a mere technical arrangement to make the new machinery work smoothly, but it was something more: it prevented the king from exercising unlimited authority. Thus the constitutional tendencies of the aristocracy, developed in earlier times, were continued by these administrative arrangements. One may hesitate to compare these achievements with modern constitutionalism, in which an unlimited power over the administration is generally given to the chief executive. But it was in fact a sort of constitutionalism, adapted to actual needs. The great battlefield of political struggle and rivalry in the seventeenth century was administration—not, as in the nineteenth century, legislation. In the administrative field constitutional law drew its lines of demarcation.

The communities and the nobility were not the only groups with whom the king had to collaborate. Long before the time of Gustavus Adolphus there had been a custom of summoning conventions of the whole realm, where nobility, clergy, burghers, and farmers could meet to consider important affairs. Since the middle of the sixteenth century these conventions have been called the riksdag, and in literature this term is traditionally used for even earlier times. Although the history of the riksdag has been very profoundly studied—especially in connection with what has been thought to be the five-hundredth anniversary of its beginning—its earlier developments are nevertheless obscure. It is certain, however, that the riksdag was frequently summoned in the third decade of the fifteenth century in connection with the struggle for liberty against the Danish kingdom, begun by that celebrated champion of liberty, Engelbrekt. From this period there is a clear line of development down to later times. Before the days of Engelbrekt, however, we have no records of any assemblies that may be characterized as riksdagar—none except the conventions that were summoned according to law, to elect kings. Furthermore, it is not likely that any such conventions occurred. It is probably correct, then, to say that the Swedish riksdag is about five hundred years old. Usually 1435 is regarded as the year of its birth, but the date is controversial.

To characterize the riksdagar of the fifteenth and sixteenth centuries as a whole, we may say that they were unknown to the law. They had, to be sure, a legal basis insofar as they presupposed that the people had rights with respect to such things as taxation, conscription, and legislation. But there were no regulations prescribing that those rights should be exercised by the people gathered in a riksdag. As a matter of fact the law prescribed no special way at all; in critical and urgent situations, however, the traditional forms could not be used. It was not enough to negotiate with that aristocratic corporation, the Council of the Realm, or with conventions of the nobility; there were other classes that could not be neglected. Neither could positive results be reached through negotiations with the different communities when the situation demanded speedy action. For entirely practical reasons, then, it was necessary to find methods of negotiation that would embrace the whole realm at once.

What questions were such conventions entitled to decide? Did they possess the legal rights of the people? Certainly not in the beginning. Legally speaking, the men who came together undertook only to persuade their communities to accept what the riksdag agreed upon; legally, therefore, the decisions made there had to be confirmed by the local communities. The riksdag, in its earliest stages, has been called merely a sort of confederation. The next step in its development was taken when the communities were persuaded to give in advance full powers to their representatives to act on their behalf. In the struggles against Catholicism at the end of the sixteenth century, representatives of the different communities were repeatedly urged to certify the adherence of their constituents by impressing the community seal on the documents containing the decisions of the riksdag. Yet, since the legal force of such an act was uncertain, the documents were sent to the communities, the clergy, and the noblemen in the different parts of the country, to be subscribed to and sealed by them also. The riksdag thus appeared not as an authority with well established rights but as an instrument to make the people themselves participate in public affairs. One is reminded of the intensive way in which the Scottish people took part in the Solemn League and Covenant of 1638. In fact the development of the riksdag in the first two centuries of its existence was accompanied, in a quite unsystematic way, by various local negotiations. Nobody could tell under what conditions a riksdag was required, and nobody could define exactly the legal effect of its decisions.

In both respects, however, the riksdag gradually grew

stronger. Being an expedient for extraordinary and urgent situations, it was important, for instance, in the fight for liberty in the last century of the Middle Ages and in the struggle with the Catholic Church at the time of the Reformation. The riksdag developed in situations where there was need for an expression of the popular will. We are often told that the executive power grows stronger in times of external difficulties and war. This is not the whole truth. Such situations promoted in Sweden the development of a self-conscious, active people. This statement is especially applicable to that remarkable period from 1594 onwards, when Sweden was engaged in the world-wide struggle between Catholicism and Protestantism. The riksdag was then summoned very often, and people began to think of it as an institution in a way incorporated in the legal order of the country. In fact several sorts of popular activity, such as legislation and taxation, were by and by thought to belong normally to the riksdag.

To be sure, the members of the riksdag did not always like to take the ultimate responsibility for its actions, but the king was anxious that its decisions should be a lawful and secure foundation for further action. In regard to this question the regeringsform of 1634 had an important word to say: nobody should have the right to oppose the decisions of a riksdag that was lawfully composed.

This brings us to the question of who the men were who came together in the riksdag. The old Council of the Realm was, traditionally, its nucleus. Then, of course, the leading political class, the nobility, belonged; according to a reform from the reign of Gustavus Adolphus, however, only the heads of the noble families, as in the House of Lords, took part in the deliberations. It must be remembered that the nobility comprised several different social elements. There were the landed aristocracy and what we may call the gentry, but there were also many people who were far from having the social position of the English gentry. The preference shown the nobility was justified by their special duties, which from the time of Gustavus Adolphus consisted above all in administrative and military service. Hence it may be said that, as members of the nobility, the heads of the civil service and the army belonged to the riksdag. The church was represented by the bishops, but also by members chosen by and from among the rectors. Special representatives were sent from the cities.

There were also the farmers. From each hundred, one farmers' representative had to be sent to the riksdag. In the sixteenth century the representatives seem, as a rule, to have been elected by the officers of the king, but since the end of that century the communities have been left to choose their representatives themselves. Moreover, we hear nothing about a limitation of the franchise in these elections; there seems to have been complete democracy. Of very great importance was the rule that the farmers, like other classes, should be represented by one of themselves. This was a consequence of the separation between the different estates of the realm, which principle prevented the farmers from being represented by, for instance, men from the landed gentry. Very often, certainly, the men who were sent to the riksdag would have liked to escape the task, the long and often dangerous journeys and the heavy responsibility to their brethren, who did not like new burdens. Nevertheless the farmers were expected to come themselves, and they did come, directly from their work— unlearned, poor men, true samples of the common people.

Remarkable elements of democracy are thus to be found in the Swedish riksdag at a time when in other countries democratic institutions were quite unknown. Members of the English Parliament would have been astonished to see what simple people had to take part in the affairs of the realm and share the responsibilities.

Nobility, clergy, burghers, and farmers formed, from the end of the sixteenth century, different houses—the four estates (*stånd*). Thus the Swedish riksdag got the peculiar structure it retained for two centuries and a half. The rights of the different houses were not as yet fixed. Quite naturally, however, the nobility claimed a degree of superiority, and the farmers were to some extent put aside. In discussions of foreign policy, for instance, they were not generally allowed to take part.

The riksdag was a powerful instrument of national policy. Again and again it gave important manifestations of a strong national will. Now it is clear to every student of political science and public law that a common will does not arise of itself, particularly not in a wide-spread country where there are few links between the populations of the different sections. The unity is, at least in great part, a product of leadership; the riksdag had its leaders. In the Middle Ages the leaders of the struggle for liberty, called the wardens of the realm, led the riksdag. When the wardenship of the last century of the Middle Ages was transformed into a national kingdom (1523), the king took over the leadership the wardens had exercised before.

Most of the Swedish kings in those times happened to have rare gifts of persuasion and also that capacity for seeing objectives and finding ways to reach them that makes the real political leader. They were really kings *in* parliament, meeting the members, talking to them, and listening to their objections and advice. Gustavus Adolphus may, in his relation to the riksdag, be compared with an English prime minister of today. He was in a sense a party leader, since he had to gather the people willing to follow him and guide them in his national program. But his party was a party of a distinct type. It might be compared, in some respects, to the state parties of the modern dictatorships, for persuasion was not the only solder that held it together. Papacy was a heresy, and those who inclined to it were not tolerated. Had anybody tried to sustain the modern ideas of free thought and speech he might have met the assertion that he was not a good citizen and that he had forgotten the fidelity he had sworn to the king. The medieval idea of fidelity and service still had a strong footing in the public opinion of those times. It was not only with the nobility, in accordance with feudal traditions, that this idea was preserved; it was an essential point in public law that the whole people, according to their oath, owed faithful service to the king. In the relations between the king and the riksdag this idea is apparent again and again in the exhortations and warnings of the king.

This moral link between leader and representatives raises the suspicion that the representative system was a camouflage. It may suggest the relations between modern dictators and their parliaments. But this is not the whole of the truth, nor even the half of it. The Swedish kings of those days could require service and loyalty from the estates, but they could not demand blind obedience, and they did not receive it. It is true that the king alone had the right to propose measures to the riksdag, but it was up to the estates to figure out how the needs that the king announced should be met—whether by taxes or conscriptions or what. The riksdag records reveal that there were clashing opinions, debates, and negotiations within the bounds of the common program.

It was in this way that the riksdag became an instrument of national policy. That sense of national unity, that consciousness of common interest, which is the indispensable basis of a sound national life was created in Sweden in times of war and difficulties; not by the commands of a powerful monarch but by the common work of free men. We are disposed to think that in this way community solidarity became more deeply rooted in our people than in many other nations in those days.

FROM THE SEVENTEENTH CENTURY
TO THE NINETEENTH

SWEDISH constitutional history is the history of the royal power and the riksdag. The country has always been governed by a king. The question of establishing a republican government has never been seriously raised. Naturally the powers actually exercised by the royalty have not always been the same. Some of the kings have been weak, others strong; some have been good, others bad. It is certain, however, that we have never since had a king with the natural gifts for popular leadership of Gustavus Adolphus and his forefathers. As there has been a king, so there has always been a riksdag. There have been times when it has depended upon the king whether the riksdag should be summoned, as was the case, in principle, in the days of Gustavus Adolphus. In such times long intervals—eight, nine, once thirteen years—might occur between the meetings. But there have been other times (1660–80, 1719–72, and since 1809) when the riksdag has had a legal right to be convened or to assemble without the king's summons, every third or fifth year. It is fair to say, then, that the riksdag has had a continuous history.

From the times of Gustavus Adolphus down to 1866 the riksdag had essentially the same structure. The four estates retained the places in public life that they received three hundred years ago. First came the nobility, who assembled in the House of the Nobles. In the seventeenth century the landed estates of the nobility increased considerably, through grants from the Crown. The heads of the aristocracy came to have a position to be compared with that of the high aristocracy in England or the petty princes in Germany. This evolution was suddenly interrupted by a financial and social revolution accomplished at the end of the seventeenth century by King Charles XI. Great tracts of land were reclaimed by the Crown. After this time the distinguishing feature of our nobility was their connection with the civil service and the army. The great mass of the men in the House of the Nobles were civil servants and army officers. To speak in the language of earlier times, they served the king and the realm both as administrative officers and as members of the riksdag.

The idea generally held in modern constitutions, that membership in parliament is incompatible with administrative service, was quite incomprehensible to our House of the Nobles. It was, of course, incomprehensible also to the bishops and rectors in the estate of the clergy, and, to a certain degree, even to the estate of the burghers—for the cities always sent many mayors as their representatives, and the mayors were administrative and legal professionals.

In the estate of the farmers there was a quite different situation. There was nothing of a bureaucracy. Yet even there we find, in a different way, the connection between administrative and parliamentary work. The farmers who were sent to Stockholm had generally grown up under local self-government. In English history it has often been observed that the House of Commons was deeply rooted in the local government of the different parts of the realm. Exactly the same observation may be made in Sweden with the great difference that in Sweden it refers not to a leading social class but to the great mass of people, the farmers. To understand how it was possible for the farmers to retain their freedom and their influence we must remember the social revolution under Charles XI, mentioned above. It secured their freedom, which had been threatened by the overwhelming position of the landed aristocracy in the middle of the seventeenth century.

So much for the composition of the riksdag. To describe its position in political life, according to constitutional laws and constitutional practice, the same summary method cannot be used, since the power of the riksdag increased and diminished several times. Different periods must therefore be distinguished. The main lines may be made clear by taking five such periods.

The first period extends from the death of Gustavus Adolphus (1632) to the accession of Charles XI (1672). This was a time when wars and foreign policy dominated national life—the most illustrious period perhaps in Swedish history, when our armies fought in Germany and Poland, and Sweden became a leading power in northern Europe. The national policy was carried on in constant collaboration with the riksdag, meeting almost every third year. It became an established rule that laws could not be made without its consent, and above all that no taxes could be raised and no conscriptions made without it. Other forms in which the people had in earlier times exercised their rights in these respects disappeared. When the riksdag was in this way constantly consulted, the self-consciousness and the pretensions of the estates increased, especially since the monarchs were for long periods under age. The Council of the Realm, acting in the name of the king, as head of the administration, could not command the same respect as the four estates constituting the riksdag. The estates took a great deal of time to debate the proposals submitted to them, and they initiated many acts themselves. It may be of some interest to observe that in the sixteen-sixties the leaders of the Council of the Realm were chosen with the consent of the riksdag. This was the first attempt to establish something similar to parliamentary government.

The second period begins with the accession of Charles XI. Through the social and financial revolution already mentioned, the high aristocracy was humiliated, and the Council of the Realm lost its prominent place. The changes were not really directed against the riksdag, but financial reorganization and peaceful times made the king less dependent on the estates than he had been before. By and by, also, theories of monarchic absolutism got a footing in Swedish political thought; the absolute power of the king was emphasized in the same way as in other monarchies of those times. In this situation the great northern war (1700–21) began. The absolute monarchy was then already so deeply rooted that Charles XII did not even once summon the riksdag during the long war.*

After his death, in 1718, however, there came a sudden change, and the so-called era of liberty (1719–72) began. The situation may be compared with that of England in 1689. Since there was no legal heir to the throne the riksdag was in the position to decide on what conditions a new monarch should be accepted. Now there was wide-spread discontent with royal omnipotence, the heavy burdens that the wars had caused, and the policy directed against the aristocracy; and the estates were anxious to restore the balance between the public powers—the king, the council, and the riksdag.

*The riksdag did meet during this period, but it was not summoned by the king.

It is very interesting to speculate upon the role political thought may have played on this occasion; the ideas of the fathers of the new constitution have, indeed, been very thoroughly studied. Some students have emphasized the role of contemporary political doctrines. As a matter of fact Locke and other writers were studied in Sweden. Others have laid more stress on the connection with the Swedish traditions and institutions before the time of absolutism; in their eyes the revolution of 1719 was above all a restoration. This question recurs at several important points in our constitutional history: has our constitution been modified by current political doctrines of wide influence, or has it developed naturally on a national basis? I think there is a great deal of truth in both views.

The constitutional laws defined several fields as within the scope of the riksdag. The consent of that body was, as in the seventeenth century, required for legislation and taxation; a remarkable novelty was that it also had to decide upon the budget. Later developments did not, however, depend merely on the particular stipulations of the constitutional laws. Of decisive importance was a theory of parliamentary omnipotence that became by and by a recognized part of our public law. The theory of the balance of power faded; it became impossible for the king or the council to vindicate their rights against those of the riksdag. There were no limits to its power; like the English Parliament, it could decide anything it pleased.

And it did. This is a notable difference between Swedish and English constitutional development. The riksdag did not hesitate to consider, according to its own views, any kind of question. There was no parliamentary leadership to make it follow the guidance of the government, the council. It displayed, as far as it could, its own faculties of thought and reasoning, not only in questions of legislation or in the broad issues of national policy but also in administrative details and other petty questions. Many questions were initiated by private members and ordinary citizens, and the riksdag and its committees readily interfered where they thought they could do good. They did not hesitate to take up questions of appropriation or appointment. They did not shrink from revising the decisions of the administrative authorities and giving orders to them in special cases. It happened also that they interfered in the work of the courts. With regard to foreign policy, the committees of the riksdag negotiated with the ministers of foreign powers and even concluded treaties. Special administrative authorities were often set up to carry out its decisions. To understand how this form of government arose one must remember among other things the bureaucratic structure of the estates, which made it natural for them to handle all sorts of administrative affairs.

Another essential feature ought to be mentioned. We did have a responsible parliamentary government of a kind. When the cabinet government was developing in practice in England a similar institution was being established by law in Sweden. The king and the council had regular meetings, where the cases brought before the government were decided. The king in council was no fiction, but a reality. In the council the king was reduced to a member among others. He might even be in a minority. The relations between the council and the riksdag were determined by two sets of rules, making the councillors depend on the confidence of the estates. The king was, first, obliged to choose his councillors from among persons proposed by the estates.

Secondly, the councillors were responsible to them. This responsibility was effected in a semijudicial way: the minutes of the council, as well as the minutes of several other authorities, were examined by a committee of the riksdag. If the policy of the council had been contrary to that of the parliamentary majority, the councillors were thought to have committed a fault deserving punishment; and the punishment consisted in their being removed from office by some committee of the riksdag. Thus, as in England, the responsibility for legality developed into that responsibility for good conduct of affairs which is the basis of parliamentarism.

In this way a sort of parliamentary government was formed, the composition of the council depending on the majority in the riksdag. The majorities changed, a typical party system developed, and the council became more and more a party government. As I have already pointed out, however, there is this remarkable difference between England and Sweden: the council in Sweden did not exercise any leadership at all. Its members were only the agents of the riksdag, and as long as the riksdag met (it might be for a year or more), its committees and the party leaders, who did not always take seats in the council, formed the real government. Only in the intervals between the riksdag meetings might the council be compared in some way with the English cabinet.

The government of the estates was supported by a good deal of enthusiasm. Its ideology, elaborated by many politicians and political speculators, had a similar hold upon men's minds to that later taken by the ideals of liberalism and parliamentarism. In many respects it was really a good government; it was a fine thing that broad groups of citizens took an active part in public affairs, and their performances were in many respects valuable—in legislation for instance.

There were, however, also dark points: the weakness of the government, especially in the foreign policy; the predominance of several private interests; and the insecurity in the field of justice. By and by, the conviction spread that the absence of checks and balances, the unlimited power of the riksdag, was a fundamental fault in the constitution. People were taught by experience that every unlimited power, whether that of a monarch or that of a parliament, must lead to the suppression of liberty. It was the same doctrine that Montesquieu developed in his celebrated book—a doctrine ardently studied in the last decades of the era of liberty. His famous ideas were in other countries a weapon against monarchical sovereignty; in Sweden they were used against parliamentary omnipotence.

By a *coup d'état* of King Gustavus III in 1772 the constitution of 1719 was overthrown and replaced by the so-called Gustavian constitution. This may be described as a somewhat romantic attempt to return to the classical state of affairs that existed in the days of Gustavus Adolphus, with its harmony between the king and the riksdag. It was also influenced by the current theories of separation of powers. As a matter of fact, however, the balance and harmony aimed at could not be maintained. There arose conflicts between the king and the riksdag, and the power of the king was extended. At the beginning of the nineteenth century Sweden was again not very far from monarchical absolutism.

THE CONSTITUTION OF 1809

By a new revolution—the last one in a constitutional history full of changes—a king whose policy had brought Sweden into serious difficulties was dethroned in 1809. The fifth and last period (1809–66) in the history of the four estates since the death of Gustavus Adolphus then began. From another point of view too the historical survey is brought to an end when we turn to a consideration of the new constitution of 1809, which was the result of the revolution, for this constitution is still in force.

When the regeringsform of 1809 was framed, the ideas of balance and division of powers once more, as in 1772 and to a certain degree as early as in 1719, dominated the public mind. Many of those who took part in framing it were imbued with the ideas of the French Revolution and familiar with the theories of Montesquieu and others. But they knew Sweden's own history too. They had fresh experiences of an unfettered monarchy, and they knew very well the consequences of parliamentary omnipotence in the era of liberty. In this way Swedish history helped to verify and corroborate the theses of Montesquieu and to emphasize the necessity of a thoroughly elaborated machinery to secure at once an independent kingship and an independent riksdag. Like the American constitution, the Swedish constitution took the idea of balance of power seriously. But the goal was not reached by adopting such arrangements as the constitution makers and political philosophers in other countries had invented. The materials, the elements of the structure, were with few exceptions taken from earlier constitutional laws—only adjusted and combined in new forms for new purposes.

The constitution of 1809 secured the rights of the riksdag in legislation, taxation, appropriation, and in some other respects. There were many safeguards also to prevent the king from interfering with the liberty of debate and decision. This does not mean however that, as according to the classical scheme of division of power, the riksdag rules alone over one part of state activity. The idea of collaboration prevails. For instance, the riksdag should not be called the legislative power, since legislation demands a joint decision of king and riksdag.

Just as the constitution makers were anxious to secure the rights of the riksdag, they also laid stress upon the limits of those rights. The king had to "govern the realm alone." This implied, among other things, that he could make certain laws without the consent of the riksdag. Moreover, the control of foreign policy was reserved to him, and the riksdag was expressly forbidden to interfere in administrative and judicial cases.

The exercise of the royal power was regulated insofar as the king, just as in the era of liberty, always had to act in his council. The old Council of the Realm, which had been abolished in 1789, was re-established as a State Council (*statsråd*). But the king had to choose its members himself, and he was obliged only to listen to their advice, not to act according to their will. Parliamentary ideas were as far from the minds of the Swedish constitutional fathers as from the American two decades earlier.

While securing in this way the independence of the executive power, the constitution at the same time (reviving to a certain extent arrangements from the eighteenth century) provided as much as possible for an effective supervision from the riksdag's side over government, administration, and judiciary. A parliamentary audit was organized. A high official elected by the riksdag, the solicitor general, supervised courts and administration and brought actions against officers who had committed faults.

The methods of supervising the State Council, that is to say the government, are especially interesting. It must be remembered that the ministers, if they may be called so, acted only as councillors, giving advice to the king. What they proposed and what the king decided were always to be registered in the minutes of the council. Now these minutes were, according to the tradition from the era of liberty, to be handed over to the so-called constitution committee of the riksdag. Thus the riksdag was able to oversee the actions of the government in all details and a firm basis was established for ministerial responsibility. The responsibility of the councillors consisted, according to the constitutional law of 1809, in their being responsible for the advice to the king as registered in the minutes. It belonged therefore to the constitution committee to raise questions of responsibility. A councillor could be sued by the committee before a special court of impeachment if he had committed offenses against the constitution. If this was not the case, and a councillor was thought to have neglected his duties otherwise, the riksdag could, on the proposal of the committee, humbly ask the king to dismiss him.

The system of checks and balances worked, on the whole, according to the intentions of its originators as long as the four estates existed, that is to say until 1866. We had really two independent powers: the king with his council, consisting mainly of bureaucrats, and the riksdag. Sometimes they worked smoothly together; sometimes there were constitutional conflicts. But it was not possible for the king to transform the constitution according to the examples of his predecessors at the end of the seventeenth and eighteenth centuries. The position of the riksdag was in many respects, certainly, strengthened, but the king did not allow it to extend its power as far as in the era of liberty. Both powers had authority enough to maintain independent positions, but neither was able to subdue the other. The situation is familiar to everybody who knows the American constitution: simply substitute a king with great personal authority and supported by all the traditions of Swedish royal power for the president, sustained by the confidence of a majority of the people.

It may be asked why, at a time when in other countries representative assemblies were gaining more and more influence, it was not possible for the Swedish riksdag, with its old traditions, to acquire a more dominant position. The answer is that it was composed in a way that made such a development very difficult.

The riksdag was not in the modern sense a true representation of the people. The estate of the farmers, with an electorate comprising without comparison the greatest part of the people, was only one of the four estates; besides, it gained only gradually full equality in political rights with the other estates. There were, moreover, considerable social elements that did not take part in the riksdag at all. It had not been so in the beginning, but when social conditions changed, the riksdag was left untouched, just as the rotten boroughs in England retained their representation in spite of the industrial revolution. The estates became

33

more and more careful of their established rights and did not want new elements to share them. The nobility, for instance, had from the beginning received mighty infusions of fresh blood: a self-made man who did good work in the administration could hope to get at last his letters patent of nobility and to take his seat in the House of the Nobles. By and by, however, ennoblement grew rarer. The nobility was transformed into a close, hereditary, privileged class. In the same way, the estate of the clergy had no room for intellectuals outside the church. Even the farmers were jealous of their rights as owners of real estate; they would not allow tenants, workmen, and others to share their political rights.

From yet another point of view the four estates did not very well answer modern demands upon a representative assembly. Their bureaucratic character, the connection between the riksdag and administration, has already been emphasized. In times when the riksdag was strong and the royal power weak, this perforce tended to weaken the royal power still more, since the king's servants in the civil service did not forget that they were also members of the riksdag. When the king was powerful, on the other hand, his administrative powers could be used to influence the civil servants in their parliamentary work. This is a counterpart to the royal influence over the House of Commons before 1832.

Finally, the very organization of the riksdag implied a weakness. It was a rather difficult thing to establish a successful collaboration between the four estates after the kings had ceased to lead their work personally. The technical difficulties were to a certain degree overcome through a system of standing committees (*utskott*), in which members of the different estates came together to prepare the measures to be taken by the riksdag. These committees, by bringing nobility, clergy, burghers, and farmers to common deliberations and an intimate exchange of views and wishes, no doubt had a very great political and social value, but their task was often hopeless. Those mighty impulses that had once made a unity of the different elements in the riksdag dwindled away more and more. The estates gradually became inclined to maintain their own rights and pretensions, and in this struggle of interests the common interests were often lost sight of.

This is the problem of every representative assembly: how to make it an organ of national policy instead of an instrument for promoting the private interests of the members and their constituencies. The well-known theory that the members of the riksdag are the representatives of the nation, not of single groups or localities, was already developed in Sweden in the eighteenth century. But we all know it is a very difficult thing to carry such a theory into practice. So when the royal leadership relaxed, there is nothing astonishing in the fact that the members of the riksdag often took care of their own special interests and those of their constituencies first. I do not imply that the Swedish riksdag was more selfish than other representative assemblies have been. This tendency, however, inherent in every representative assembly, to regard the public power as an instrument for promoting private interests, was accentuated by the four-chamber system of Sweden; it became a sort of public duty to vindicate the interests of the different estates, one against the other. Sweden has really had valuable experience in the difficulties of so-called functional or organic representation.

35

In this way the question of reforming the representative system, in one way or another, became urgent. The development of representative institutions in other countries emphasized the need for reform. In comparison with the English Parliament, the French Chambers, the American Congress, and those representative bodies created by our Scandinavian neighbors in the first half of the nineteenth century, Sweden's riksdag looked like an odd remnant from ancient times. Such a judgment was perhaps unjust insofar as it lead to underestimating what our riksdag had been— a precursor of representative government at a time when nobody in other countries, except England, thought of such a thing. But it was quite natural; class representation could not continue. In 1866 therefore, three decades after the reform bill in England, our reform bill was passed, abolishing the four estates.

THE RIKSDAG OF TODAY

IN ACCORDANCE with the political ideas prevailing at the middle of the nineteenth century, the four estates were in 1866 replaced by a bicameral system. The First Chamber corresponds to the Senate or House of Lords; the Second Chamber is more truly representative of the people.

The Second Chamber had in the beginning the stamp of middle-class liberalism. The franchise rules practically excluded the workingmen's class from the vote. Small owners of real estate were more liberally admitted to the polls, and the farmers gained a very strong footing in the Second Chamber. They formed a Farmers' party, which comprised in the eighties, for example, not far from half the members of the chamber. Other members formed smaller groups or joined no group at all.

The idea that parties are an indispensable element of political life gained ground only slowly. Parties, in the sense of organizations to organize the elections, scarcely appeared before the nineties, and statistics tell us that the interest taken in elections was comparatively small. At the beginning of the twentieth century people were still rather generally convinced that the highest duty of a representative was to decide cases brought before him according to his own judgment, not according to party lines. The liberal idea that representatives should be really independent people survived for a comparatively long time.

In the first decade of the twentieth century all this changed. The workingmen's class increased considerably and demanded its share in public affairs. It was organized as a Socialist party in 1889, and as a consequence other ideas and movements also took the form of party organizations embracing electors as well as representatives. In 1907 universal suffrage was carried through; proportional representation was established at the same time, as a concession to the Conservatives, who were afraid of losing all their influence. The reform was carried through by a Conservative cabinet, but as a matter of fact it was mainly due to the efforts of the Liberal party. It also gave this party a commanding influence in the Second Chamber. Very soon, however, the Liberals had to share the common European fate of liberal parties and give place to others. In the period between 1914 and 1936 we had an equilibrium between the four main parties, none of which possessed a majority: the Conservatives, the Liberals, the Farmers' party, and the Socialists. Finally, the elections in 1936 gave the Socialist party nearly a majority. Having been joined by some members of a semi-communistic party, it has now exactly half the membership of the Second Chamber (115 out of 230). Its position is strengthened even further by close cooperation with another class party, the Farmers.

Notable as this dominance of the Socialists is in itself—for there are few examples of Socialist parties having absolute majorities—it is also a new experience for us, since never before has any party held such a position in our riksdag. In earlier times the independence of the representatives made for shifting majorities on the various questions. So it was, too, when we had a number of parties, which had to combine with one another to accomplish their objectives. Now for the first time we have, as England does, a fairly stable division between a ruling majority and an ineffectual minority, the votes of which usually have no weight at all. The importance of this situation is enhanced by the fact that there is stronger discipline in the Socialist party than in the others. The predominating questions to-day are: will the Socialist party be able to maintain its solidarity in spite of the many different interests and ideas it embraces? And will it be able to retain its majority?

The First Chamber is elected proportionally by municipal representative bodies: the provincial councils and the councils of the six largest cities. Members are elected for a term of eight years, one-eighth of the members being elected every year. The original municipal franchise regulations made the First Chamber a very plutocratic body. This created a tension between the two chambers, heightened all the more by the fact that the constitutional laws had given them equal powers. A fundamental idea in the reform of 1866 was the aim of establishing a real balance between the chambers. In the catch phrases of the reformers, the American bicameral system, not the English one, should be the model.

With the growth of democratic feeling Sweden was confronted with this familiar question about the First Chamber, or upper house: should it remain unreformed and lose part of its influence, or should it be transformed in some way? An answer was first given in 1907 by a comparatively thoroughgoing democratization, which, however, still left the majority to the Conservatives. This step was not enough to satisfy the Liberals and Socialists, and in December, 1918, under the overwhelming influence of the constitutional changes going on in Central Europe, the First Chamber was completely transformed. It is now based on practically the same franchise regulations as the Second Chamber, the main difference being that the First Chamber is elected indirectly, for a longer period, and with partial annual renewal. The result is that there is now no broad gulf between the chambers, although changes in popular opinion are reflected more slowly in the First Chamber. For instance, the First Chamber still has (1938) a non-Socialist majority. This may, however, change very rapidly; the municipal councils that elect the members have been renewed this autumn (1938); since the Socialists were victorious in these elections, we reckon that in a few years there will be a Socialist majority in the First Chamber too.

How should the present position of the First Chamber be described? There are different opinions on the role it ought to play and the influence it ought to exert, but on the whole it may be said to have retained the place given it by the constitution. Generally speaking, questions are examined with equal thoroughness in both chambers; and very seldom does a member of the First Chamber shrink from acting according to his own views out of regard for the opinions prevailing in the Second Chamber, as being a more immediate expression of the popular will. Our bicameral system is still effective. Of course the cases where the chambers disagree are comparatively rare, since the proportion of the parties does not, as I have already pointed out, differ very much. Moreover, a special spirit within the Liberal group of the First Chamber, for example, is not likely to arise, because the riksdag parties are organized as single units, each of them containing members from both chambers.

To give a more complete idea of the riksdag some important facts should be added. We have an elaborate election system, giving the best guarantees for liberty in voting and an honest count. The distribution of seats among the constituencies is frequently revised to give full equality. Nobody seriously questions that the riksdag is really a true representation of the popular will; minor parties have, however, complained of being somewhat handicapped by the proportional system.

Among the representatives there are naturally many who have made politics a sort of profession. Parliamentary work in itself certainly does not give one enough to do, for it lasts only about five months every year; and few people would be content with the modest salary (seven hundred and fifty to one thousand dollars) paid to representatives. But to their parliamentary activity many representatives add other forms of political work, in party organizations, parliamentary commissions, and administrative boards, so that they become in a sense professional politicians. This is not, however, the rule. The great majority of representatives have not lost their connection with private life and work; they are really laymen spending only part of their time in parliament.

It may be of some interest to raise the question how far, from a social point of view, representatives correspond to the social structure of the community as a whole. This question must indeed be expected from anyone who is aware of all the circumstances that may make a representative assembly differ so much from the people represented. Of course we cannot expect to see the social structure reflected perfectly in the riksdag: representatives will always stand, on an average, higher than the mass of the people. But not very much higher! The riksdag is really a rather good reflection of the people, with their different professions and interests. This state of affairs is traditional in Sweden; there has never been a particular political class monopolizing

41

all political work. It was always considered important that the different classes should be represented by their own men. Thus the riksdag has always contained a great many real farmers, for instance; they still make up between thirty-five and forty per cent of the Second Chamber and more than twenty per cent of the First Chamber. Labor, too, is to a large extent represented by real workers; in the Second Chamber they are about thirteen per cent of the whole number. We are justified in adding to this percentage many representatives who are officers of trade-unions, newspapermen, inferior civil servants, and so on, but who are nevertheless closely in touch with the working class, in many respects feeling and thinking as the workers do. There are very few people in the riksdag who may be regarded as capitalists in a proper sense. Since in Sweden one is not expected to spend one's own money in election campaigns, parties need not seek candidates among the rich.

Just as in earlier days, many members of the riksdag are at the same time administrative officers. There is nothing to prevent civil servants from being elected. Their proportionate number in the riksdag is far from being as great as in earlier times, but it is certainly not negligible. Some civil servants play a rather considerable role, at times in opposition to the government. While in this way there is brought to the riksdag a good deal of experience from state administration, the connection between parliamentary and municipal work has also been maintained, and representatives often come to the riksdag with rich experience in municipal life.

Representatives, as a whole, enjoy general respect. Of course they are also criticized. One often hears that they do not display all the ability one could want, and also that they are sometimes inclined to place private interests above the common good. As a whole, however, the chambers maintain a standard we cannot in justice complain of.

In the organization of parliamentary work some features may be observed that differ from ordinary bicameral schemes. The two chambers had certainly no root at all in Swedish traditions, but it is quite natural that their organization and their forms of action should in many respects resemble those of the old riksdag. The *riksdagsordning,* or constitutional law that regulates the organization of the riksdag, often shows connections with the order existing before 1866; many traditions from the eighteenth and even from the seventeenth century still survive in Swedish parliamentary life.

The committee (*utskott*) system should above all be emphasized. In the old riksdag committees were primarily responsible for coordinating the four estates, and were, therefore, composed of members from all of them. Without such organs it would scarcely have been possible to harmonize the vigorous wills of the different estates. This joint committee system was so deeply rooted that in 1866 it was simply transplanted to the new riksdag. There are also of course some committees of the common type, established by each chamber separately; but they play a very insignificant role. As a rule committees are common to both chambers, i. e., joint committees, half of the members being chosen by a proportional vote of each chamber. In earlier times, when there was generally a broad breach between the chambers, committees did much to bridge it. The rich people and high officials from the First Chamber came to be on speaking terms with the farmers from the Second, and many useful compromises were made between positions that might seem to be irreconcilable. Although today there is not the same need for an instrument of conciliation, the organization is left untouched. The First Chamber continues to exercise its power not only through decisions in opposition to those of the Second Chamber, but in the first instance through its members' influence in committee deliberations. The committees are generally standing committees (*ständiga utskott*). Constitutional law defines the sphere of action of each of them, and most of the members are reelected year after year, thus gaining a considerable amount of experience and authority in the subjects entrusted to them.

A remarkable and peculiar consequence of the system of joint committees is that, as a rule, both chambers have to decide questions at the same time. This arrangement is thought to be a guarantee for the equality of the chambers, neither of them taking precedence. It also, however, entails a loss of opportunity for reconsideration, which usually is possible in other countries where questions are sent from one chamber to another. Now, when the difference between the chambers no longer retards decisions and makes them difficult, the absence of such a natural check upon impulsive or precipitate decisions is sometimes to be regretted.

The position of the committees is a strong one—it should be borne in mind that they have traditions going back to the eighteenth if not to the seventeenth century. Every question put before the riksdag, whether it comes from the government or from private members, has to be examined by a committee; and this examination is far from being merely formal. A comparison of the committees with those of the American Congress is not unjustifiable. In most cases the committees' decisions are accepted by the riksdag.

Perhaps I ought, however, to warn against an exaggerated notion of the influence of the committees. The members of the committees are not dictators. They usually work in close touch with their parties, and in important questions it often happens that the parties make a preliminary decision before the committee settles the question. Thus the importance of the committees consists rather more in their being instruments for making the opinions of the parties clear and definite than in the mere personal influence of the members in matters committed to them.

The work of the chambers has not become merely formal either. They spend much time in debate—some people say too much, and add that the representatives often speak more to the public than to the fellow members of the chamber. Of course debate does not have all the power for clarifying issues that earlier liberalism ascribed to it; but the traditional confidence in the value of discussion is strong enough—rooted as it is not only in the ideas of modern liberalism but also in a much older national tradition—to prevent any attack on freedom of speech in the riksdag. Having no restrictions at all on freedom of debate has put us to no serious inconveniences. Obstruction is unknown, as far as I have observed, and I think that any member who tried it openly would meet with practically unanimous disapproval and contempt.

PARLIAMENTARY GOVERNMENT

In DESCRIBING the organization of the riksdag and its methods of working, I have not as yet touched upon a question of fundamental importance, its relations to the government. Some of the technicalities of organization and procedure are of little interest unless they are seen in this relationship.

Does Sweden have a responsible parliamentary government or not? Let us recall the constitutional basis of the question. The king is according to the constitution not only a reigning but a governing monarch. He has to make decisions; his councillors (*statsråd*), who are chosen by him, only have to give him their advice. He is not expected to inquire whether they have the confidence of the riksdag or not. Yet in practice, in reality, Sweden does have a parliamentary government.

In the first place, it is a long time since the king made use of his right to decide without being in accord with his councillors. A councillor is never asked to countersign a decision he does not approve. Thus the system of government in Sweden has changed from the type that is characteristic of the American constitution to the system that prevails generally in constitutional and parliamentary governments.

Secondly, the king has felt more and more fettered in his choice of councillors. Even Charles John (1818–44), the founder of the Bernadotte dynasty, discovered that a deadlock between the two powers that our constitution requires to cooperate could best be avoided by calling into the council persons with a strong position in the riksdag, in the hope of winning its confidence. In a representative body so divided and so zealous for personal independence as ours was in earlier times, such prospects were, however, rather uncertain; and the riksdag, when no stable majorities arose, could scarcely expect the king to follow parliamentary lines in his choice. After 1866 however the parliamentary situation brightened. The Farmers' party had a program that could have been made the basis for a parliamentary government. But it was congressionalistic in its tendencies, zealous for the rights of the riksdag, and did not care for ministerial positions and responsibility. In the period between 1866 and 1905, as a matter of fact, an increasing number of influential members of parliament took places in the council together with high bureaucrats, and since the seventies such men have nearly always filled the post of prime minister. But this was as much due to the wishes of the king to assure an effective government as to any desire on the part of the riksdag to create a parliamentary system.

The Liberal party was the first to demand, at the very beginning of the twentieth century, a parliamentary government according to the English model. The principle was not accepted at once; the Conservatives maintained the prerogatives of the king, and the Socialists hesitated to share the ministerial responsibility. Since 1905 however we have had, as a rule, governments more or less directly sustained by some party or party combination. By 1920 the parliamentary principle had become generally accepted, even by the king, who had as late as 1914 formed a rather successful royal cabinet. But at the very moment when the principle was accepted, its traditional ground wavered. There were no parties possessing an absolute majority, and the Liberal party, which had the key position, was never willing, although the king constantly urged them, to give up their special aims to form a majority combination. Thus the Liberals, at the moment when their ideas were victorious in the minds of the people, were themselves the obstacle to the realization of those ideas. And Sweden, in common with many other countries in the years after the war, got the system that has taken its name from English parliamentarism but is very far from its spirit—the so-called minority parliamentarism. Liberal, Conservative, and Socialist cabinets quickly succeeded one another. There was always a change after a general election and very often between them. The choice between the parties that could be considered capable of forming a cabinet depended, of course, upon the actual relations between the parties; frequently two different solutions appeared equally feasible. The cabinets consisted in large part of members of the riksdag and were usually headed by party leaders. They worked in close contact with their parties and received good support from them, but to get a majority vote they had always to negotiate with other parties.

The successes of the Socialist party in recent years, and its close cooperation since 1933 with the Farmers' party, have offered new possibilities for establishing governments according to parliamentary ideals. A Socialist cabinet, formed in 1932, was so closely in touch with the Farmers, from 1933 on, and had such a strong position in the riksdag, that it looked very like a true parliamentary cabinet. After a strange interlude in 1936, when the Farmers formed their own cabinet for a short time, the elections of the same year resulted in a cabinet based on the Socialist and Farmers' parties together, headed by the Socialist party leader and commanding a strong majority. Today for the first time we have a cabinet that really has the confidence of a majority in both chambers.

Shall we say then that the English method of forming cabinets has been introduced into Sweden? It is perhaps too early to answer. Indispensable elements of the classical English system are the sensitiveness of the electorate, its readiness to react to the mistakes of the cabinet, and its parliamentary majority. It is a question whether such reactions are to be expected from the Socialist voters, many of whom are closely connected to their party by personal allegiance and loyalty. Many people believe that the men who are now governing our country, or at any rate the Socialists, will remain in power for a very long time. That their cooperation with the Farmers will continue seems more doubtful, especially if the Socialists should gain an absolute majority in both chambers.

From what has been said it may be concluded that it has not been the chief aim of our parliamentary majorities to gain influence over the executive power in the ways of parliamentarism. On the other hand, the riksdag has taken a great interest in strengthening its own position as a deliberative and legislative body, and the effort has been extremely successful. This is not, or at any rate only to a very small extent, due to changes in constitutional law. It is mainly a question of practice. Constitutional law is always more or less ambiguous, capable of manifold interpretation. Our constitutional laws from the beginning of the nineteenth century have been so too. Now in the large margin left to interpretation, those constructions based on the original ideas of a balance between king and people have gradually given way, in general, to those agreeing with the

49

general ideas dominating the nineteenth century, namely, the sovereignty of the people and parliamentary predominance. It is unnecessary to discuss the details of the development, so familiar to every student of political science and constitutional law. By way of illustration only it could be mentioned that the sphere in which the king may legislate independently has shrunk to nearly nothing; that he has ceased to exercise his legislative veto; and that the right of the riksdag to vote the budget has been used to prescribe the details of public expenditure.

The riksdag has won as wide a realm as it had in the era of liberty, and the popular opinion is that it may decide almost any question whatever in the field of legislation and administration. The king and the cabinet are thought of as having only as much power as the riksdag will allow them. There are, however, differences between our time and the era of liberty. The riksdag may, for instance, regulate in detail the organization of an administrative department, and it generally does; but it does not claim to influence the recruitment of the civil service or to decide current affairs belonging to the administration. To this extent the idea of the separation of powers has had a lasting hold on constitutional life. Neither does the riksdag meddle at all with questions belonging to the courts of law.

A theory of parliamentary omnipotence may, however, be compatible with a strong influence on the part of the government. Everyone knows in general what the sovereignty of parliament means in England. How is it, then, with the relations between cabinet and riksdag, with the influence of the cabinet upon parliamentary work in Sweden?

The government has several legal possibilities of influence at its disposal. It has a formal right to initiate measures. Since 1866 its members have been allowed to take part in the deliberations of the chambers, while on the other hand they are as a rule excluded from committees. It also has the right to dissolve the chambers. The government initiative is of very great importance. The riksdag cannot itself, for example, make the investigations necessary for legislation and appropriation. The committees do not have time enough in a five months' session to examine thoroughly all questions put before them, and between the meetings the riksdag has no organs at its disposal. So *par la force des choses* the government, whether it be in harmony with the riksdag or not, can always expect to carry a great many of its proposals, as a matter of course.

This observation is, nevertheless, very far from deciding the whole problem. The great question is this: how does the riksdag use the time and the psychological forces it commands? How far does it use them to control affairs itself, to form a will distinct from that of the cabinet? The necessary legal powers for it to make such a contribution to public life are not lacking. Private members are entitled to raise any question, independently or as amendments to government bills. Every proposal they make, as well as those coming from the cabinet, must be examined by the committees.

The riksdag, in the period before parliamentarism was established, made use of these possibilities as a matter of course. This is quite natural, considering the congressionalistic traditions of our parliament, which rested not only on greed for power but also on a sense of personal responsibility. It was always felt to be a duty for members of parliament to judge the questions put before them according to their own experiences and convictions. This trend was perhaps particularly natural in a parliament where many members were trained in state administration and local government. Consequently the proposals of the cabinet were carefully examined. The committees and the chambers did not hesitate to study the texts of bills thoroughly and to alter them, or to investigate the financial proposals closely. It did not occur to the riksdag that it could not say "no" as well as "yes." Such an idea would have been in apparent contradiction with the duty of the members generally acknowledged, to judge independently the questions brought before them and to solve them according to their own convictions. There were no party links to modify this principle in favor of the government. The nonparliamentary cabinets were not allowed to lead the riksdag. The ministers could not expect to carry all their proposals; far from that. They even had to acquiesce when, at the proposal of private members, the riksdag went independently on its own way, as it very often did. Did not the right of dissolution do anything to strengthen the position of a cabinet? Not very much. The governments of those days, rather unpolitical as they were, could expect but little from an election, although it did happen once that the Second Chamber was dissolved and that the subsequent new elections were favorable to the government.

In the period from 1905 to 1936 the position of the government was strengthened insofar as it could generally rely on the support of its own party. Apart from this it was an advantage from the point of view of the cabinet that most of its members now belonged to the riksdag and were able in many ways to work upon their fellow legislators, even those of other parties. At the same time the consolidation of the party system gave rise to new difficulties. If the cabinet had a majority in one of the chambers it had either to acquiesce in the resistance of the other or to make compromises. If it commanded only a minority in both chambers (as was the case from 1920 to 1936), its position was still weaker, for its chances to control political developments depended then on its relations to the other parties and on the number of votes it had to win in every case to carry a majority. The government never had the authority an English cabinet can claim, as being supported by a popular vote. The independence of the riksdag could not be seriously threatened by menaces of resignation. There were no generally accepted principles as to the duty of a majority that had overthrown a cabinet to form a new government. The Liberal cabinets were relatively strong, because of their key position, and so were the Socialist cabinets, because they were not far from having a majority and could often procure the small number of supporters they needed from other parties. For the Conservative cabinets, however, it was very difficult to put through, even approximately, their own program. In any case, the cabinet was very, very far from the position of an English cabinet.

Thus the decisions of the riksdag generally differed considerably from what the government had proposed. The center of political gravity lay without any doubt in the riksdag, which retained its old position as an independent body, with its own thoughts and its own will. And the policy of the country was not decided by a government accomplishing its own program in all important points, but by the shifting majorities formed in the chambers. The system had its apparent inconveniences but I am inclined to think it was valuable, insofar as a system of changing majorities, in which every member and every party has a chance to take part in a majority (at any rate in some questions), is a greater integrating force than a system in which minorities are permanently destined to a merely negative position.

Now, since 1936, everything has changed. The present government has a stronger position than a Swedish government has had since the days of Gustavus Adolphus, I should say. At its first meetings with the riksdag, in 1937 and 1938, it suffered very few and inconsiderable reverses. The majority coalition voted nearly everything the cabinet proposed and not very much more. The Swedish people have not yet had time to make themselves at home with this new situation. To many people it looks like the beginning of dictatorship; they are not familiar with the English constitutional system and are perhaps inclined, in view of the strong leadership exercised there, to regard it as a somewhat dictatorial form of government. It is, of course, too early to form definite judgments. Freedom of discussion is still unlimited; private members can still expect serious consideration and public discussion of their proposals; and nobody has even a thought of giving the cabinet such powers in conducting the work of the riksdag as the English cabinet has. Perhaps the old tradition that the riksdag ought to be a really thinking and acting body will be strong enough to prevent its becoming only an instrument for debates, criticism, and expression of the policy of the government.

Finally, what is, after all these changes, the actual position of the Crown? The question has already in large part been answered. The king, like most monarchs in modern times, has ceased to govern. On the other hand, his symbolic functions have become more and more apparent—though I hesitate to characterize the public appearance of the

Crown as only symbolic. I think especially of our Crown Prince: with his broad vision and capacity for taking an interest in all sorts of social and civic efforts and for convincing others of their value, he has won a unique position, embodying the will and the sentiments of the people independent of party opinions. It is a saying that should Sweden become a republic, the Crown Prince would be sure to be elected president.

It must also be added that in the procedure of government the king plays a peculiar role, owing to the strange requirements of our constitution. As previously stated, the king has to decide in council after listening to the advice of his councillors, the cabinet. The councillors are not entitled to act independently on behalf of the Crown. This means that every question the ministers have to decide must be brought before the king. He certainly does not act against the ministers, but he has a good opportunity for influencing them, and I think that in foreign policy his advice is of no little importance. At any rate he may follow the government's work in every detail. The ministers are bound to perform their work in such a way that they can answer for the king, just as they are exposed to the critics in the constitution committee of the riksdag, which examines the minutes of the council. These are not insignificant checks on ministerial omnipotence.

STATE ADMINISTRATION

PUBLIC administration in Sweden is traditionally composed of two distinct elements: state administration and municipal administration. These should be studied separately because each possesses a characteristic structure. State administration has the civil service as its personnel basis. Civil servants are appointed by the government or by other superior authorities, and form a hierarchic system with the king as its head. The civil service is, in principle, a profession—life-long and nonpolitical. Municipal government,* on the contrary, is in principle entrusted to laymen, who are elected, often on party lines, for a short period, and who are not supposed to devote more than part of their time to municipal affairs. In municipal administration there are, of course, persons in positions comparable to those of civil servants, but they are as a rule subordinate to the laymen.

We must not, however, lose sight of recent interesting innovations in the field of public administration that do not come within the traditional scheme, or conform to traditional types. These will be discussed in a later chapter.

To understand the character of our state administration some historical observations are necessary. The reader will remember how it was created in the seventeenth century mainly as a device for a free cooperation of the nobility with the king. Later its position changed; the nobility had

*The term *local government* should be avoided in describing Swedish institutions. There are local organs that form a part of state administration and have nothing to do with municipal government.

to give way more and more to other social elements. But the traditions survived. Our administration retained much of that relative independence it had had from the beginning. The position of the administrative departments may be compared with the position held in other countries by the courts. Until 1789 the administrative organization was regulated by constitutional laws, and as a rule administrative officers like judges could not be removed by the king. In this way we had traditionally a balance of powers within the executive branch. It was thought that liberty, security, and justice might be secured better by officers not wholly dependent on the king and therefore more likely to display in their work something of that objectivity and cautiousness generally expected from the judges; the judiciary was never thought to be the sole safeguard of justice. That this system was continued was in some degree due to the fact already mentioned, that civil servants played a considerable role in the riksdag, which thus came to take a keen interest in maintaining the independence of the administration. The efforts to assert the liberty of the riksdag were in a way combined with the interest of preserving an independent administration and thereby limiting the freedom of action of the head of the executive government.

The civil servant in Sweden is a nonpolitical professional. As such he is not supposed to represent any special political opinion or any party standpoint. Civil servants are never elected by a popular vote, but always appointed by their administrative superiors, sometimes the king in council, sometimes other authorities. The appointments are expected to be made without party considerations. There are only a very few high offices that may be regarded as political. I do not deny that in other cases, too, the ministers may consider the political views of the persons they appoint. Some people tell you that the government often does. But the government would never admit it; it is difficult for a minister to meet the criticisms that would be heard, should an obviously and admittedly political appointment be made. As a matter of fact the cases where a political purpose is evident are not frequent. The Socialist government has appointed fourteen governors of provinces. Only six of them have been Socialists, and three have belonged to a party at political enmity with the Socialists. I am not, however, quite sure that the tradition will be maintained to its full extent. In some instances we have seen new tendencies, and perhaps, if we should retain for a long time the powerful government we now have, political considerations will determine appointments more often than in the past.

The nonpolitical character of the civil service does not mean, however, that the civil servant is expected to have no political conviction or even that he must abstain from party politics. In his service he is supposed to be scrupulously unpolitical, but outside he enjoys full civic rights. He may be active in party work, he may take part in municipal government, and he may be elected a member of the riksdag. To be sure, there may be conflicts between the political interests of a civil servant and his official duties, but it is supposed that in such situations the deep-rooted tradition that a civil servant should act impartially, without personal or party considerations, will be strong enough to resolve all difficulties.

The civil servant has a life-long position. Speaking more exactly, he is allowed to retain his office until he is entitled to a retiring allowance, which is usually at the age of sixty-five. This is a fundamental principle in Swedish public law.

He is supposed to devote his life to the public service, and the state in return will grant him security. Even if his office should be suppressed he has an inviolable right to his salary. Obviously this state of affairs is not maintained only in the interest of civil servants; it is expected that the independent status granted to them will attract able people who would not take the risk of an insecure and dependent position. There are, of course, exceptions to the rule. Many employees in subordinate positions, "non-ordinary civil servants," may be dismissed; in most cases, however, they can hope sooner or later to reach the typical civil servant status. There are also a few high officers appointed for a fixed period, and others that may be dismissed when the king in council wishes, but even these officers generally remain in their offices until they have reached the age of sixty-five. Thus, when a civil servant has once been appointed to an office he can as a rule expect to retain it for life—if he is not advanced to a higher one. We are quite unfamiliar with that type of civil servants who serve for a time and then go back to private life.

As to recruitment, it happens that what I may call laymen are appointed to high offices. Sometimes prominent politicians, engineers, industrialists, and so on, are placed in leading posts in central administration or are appointed governors, but this is—or was till a few years ago—an exception. When civil servants are described as professionals, this means that they are expected either to have special knowledge before they enter the service or to acquire that knowledge by going gradually from lower offices to higher ones. The knowledge required on entering the civil service is generally won by university studies and verified by some university examination. There are few examples of reaching high offices without such examinations. The study of law plays a very important role in this respect. In the central administration and in the governors' departments most high offices are occupied by lawyers who have behind them the same university studies as judges and barristers. This is a deep-rooted tradition reflecting the idea that administrative departments as well as courts have to handle public affairs in a spirit of justice and impartiality. Some people think we have too much juridical training and thinking in our administration and should have more representation of economics, statistics, political science, and similar studies. A few years ago a new form of examinations was instituted to remedy this defect, but it remains to be seen whether the traditional composition of the civil service will be essentially altered in this way. It should be mentioned that the organization of legal studies traditionally pays regard to the fact that lawyers have to meet the needs not only of the courts and the bar but also of state administration.

The methods of recruitment have, as a matter of fact, never presented any serious problems. It is a well established principle that civil servants should be appointed and promoted with respect to their actual merits; the constitution provides that in appointments and promotions only "merits and ability" should be considered. We have no special recruitment offices to carry this rule into execution; the choice is left entirely to the appointing authorities themselves. But as a matter of fact the appointment and promotion machinery works on the whole objectively and justly. Of course the Swedish high officials are not angels, and since they are not they have friends and favorites and children and cousins whose welfare they are tempted to promote. Those who have no such connection with the mighty are therefore sometimes dissatisfied, but there are remarkable safeguards against arbitrary and unfair appointments. In many cases we have rather precise provisions as to the qualifications required for different services, and the administrative authorities as a rule develop somewhat rigid principles as to the value of different examinations and long experience in office. It is of no little importance that there is public competition for most posts in the civil service: a vacant post is publicly advertised, and anyone has an opportunity to apply for it. There is also supervision by superior authorities; one who fails to get an appointment can always appeal to the king in council, and very often does.

The control of the people through public opinion should also be mentioned. The public has, owing to peculiar arrangements I am going to describe later, an excellent opportunity to follow what is going on in appointment and promotion practice. The public takes a great interest in such affairs and is very much inclined to react against wrong steps. Perhaps, in this concern for justice in personnel administration, we sometimes pass from Scylla to Charybdis: a man who is thought to have a right to an office because of high university honors and good testimonials may be preferred to one who is really the better man for the job.

As to the legal status of the civil servants, some salient features must be set forth. The administration forms a hierarchy in which one is superior, another subordinate. There seems to be no doubt that the Swedish state administration can be described, according to American terminology, as wholly integrated. But this natural dependence is not so pronounced as it is in the administration of most other countries; for this reason, that the idea of subordination is modified by the principle that a civil servant must act on his own responsibility, according to the prescriptions of law. It is, to be sure, no easy task to describe exactly the legal consequences of this principle. It does not mean that the subordinate officer is not subject to the orders of superiors; for in many situations he is. But he is expected to have his own opinions, not to be a tool in the hands of his superiors. To give but one illustration, a civil servant is not, according to prevailing opinion, subject to orders from his superiors as to the interpretation and the application of a statute; he has to have his own opinion on its meaning and to bear the responsibility for the way in which he carries it out. This refers, of course, mainly to those fields of administration in which legal questions arise, and especially to those in which the administration has to do with the rights of the citizens. In merely technical departments, where the exigencies of efficiency must prevail, the subordination is more strongly pronounced.

As the power of superiors is, in principle, restricted, their means for influencing subordinates indirectly are also limited. They may inflict disciplinary punishments, but not on all civil servants; the higher ones are exempted. Furthermore the exercise of this power is under the control of an independent administrative court. Since civil servants are irremovable they need not fear that they will be dismissed if their work does not please their superiors. According to Swedish constitutional law civil servants are also protected against transfer from one post to another. Recent legislation has, however, made various exceptions to this rule, which has been thought to be too great an obstacle to the effective organization of the civil service, especially in those departments that are mainly technical. In other departments this power of the government to transfer officers has not yet been used to any considerable extent.

If civil servants are more independent of their superiors than is usually the case in modern administration, they are on the other hand responsible for their actions to the general courts and, let me say, to public opinion also.

An officer who has failed to discharge his functions properly may be prosecuted before the general courts. This is of very great importance, for our criminal code has, in a general clause, made a crime out of all the failures a civil servant may be responsible for: every act proving "negligence, omission, want of judgment, or want of skill." Thus a civil servant is always bound to consider those points of view from which a court is likely to judge his work. The solicitor general, who is elected every year by the riksdag, provides, as a sort of *tribunus plebis,* for making this control by the courts effective. There is also a special solicitor general who supervises military officers.

Still more interesting is another arrangement. The documents in the administrative offices are, in principle, public. Anyone can demand that they be produced. In this way we have sought to attain a public control over administration that may be compared to the control over the courts that derives from the fact that their sessions are public. Public opinion, with its demand for justice and honesty, is expected to be and really is a power that civil servants must always take into consideration. The documents that form the basis for administrative decisions are always accessible to the public, and especially to the newspapers, and so are the decisions. The officer who is tempted to act arbitrarily, or to let private interests influence his decisions, must always risk a public discussion based on exact knowledge of the case. There are naturally many exceptions to this rule—the Foreign Office, for example, is not bound to open its records—but the rule is far-reaching enough to affect, in a decisive way, the behavior of public administration.

This hasty survey may have revealed that our state administration has a spirit of its own, a sense for legality and responsibility—something of that consciousness which may be observed in many countries in the judiciary. It goes without saying that the public service enjoys general esteem and that the social position of civil servants is high. The work of a civil servant is thought to be a lifework fitting for able, independent people who take an interest in public affairs.

The organization of state administration, like the status of civil servants, has certain distinctive characteristics. Some of these have enough general interest to warrant emphasis.

In most countries the central administration is organized as a system of instruments or machinery at the disposal of the ministers and under their immediate direction. This does not, however, accurately describe Swedish institutions. Legally speaking we have had, since the seventeenth century, two distinct elements in central administration: the king with his councillors, and a number of separate boards or government offices, each headed by a high officer from the civil service, a director general. We have, for instance, the Board of Army Administration, the Board of Naval Administration, the Board of Audit, the Post Office, the Railways Office, the Social Welfare Board, the Medical

Attendance Board, the School Board, and others. For nearly all fields of administration there are such central offices (*centrala verk*).

The structure of the central offices is as a rule determined by the riksdag's appropriations. The riksdag traditionally takes a great interest in the organization of administrative departments, which is not at all thought to be one of the prerogatives of the government. As a matter of fact the organization of the central offices is rather rigid. In most cases the director general has to make the decisions in the name of the office after he has heard the advice of a *chef de bureau*. In many important matters, however, and especially when the decisions will affect the rights of citizens, the director general and some *chefs de bureau* together form a board that decides by a majority vote. Appeal cases, for instance, are to a great extent decided in this way.

The functions of central administration are divided between the government and the central offices. This division is regulated by the government, which reserves matters of greater importance for itself and leaves current affairs to the offices. The demarcation is always made in a general way, and although it is, of course, subject to alterations, it tends to be permanent. Thus each central office comes to feel a deep responsibility for good conduct of public affairs in the sphere entrusted to it. By long experience it develops its own viewpoints, its own principles. Some of the offices have had a long time to form their own traditions; there are offices that date from the seventeenth century. Some years ago one of them, the Chamber College, when asked by the government to give its opinion on some legal questions regarding a certain real estate, merely referred to its report of August 29, 1692. This was not far from a joke, of course, but it may serve to elucidate the continuity in the work of the central offices.

The independence of the central offices does not mean that they are not subordinate to the king, however. They are, like all administrative departments, subject to his leadership (this leadership means nowadays as a matter of fact the leadership of a parliamentary government). But the departments are not subject to the directions of a minister. A minister has, legally speaking, to give advice to the king, but is not to make decisions himself. He is not allowed to say to the chief of an office, to its director general: "Please appoint Mr. A.; please give that job to Mr. B.; please give a loan to that company, a license to that man." He cannot even indicate the general principles for deciding a certain sort of cases. And since he is not responsible for the work of the offices, he will not as a rule be inclined to meddle with their activity, at all events not in subjects where no political questions are at issue. He may, of course, procure a decision of the king in council prescribing what a central office ought to do; but although the king never will refuse his consent, this is not the same thing as giving orders informally by talking or telephoning to the director general. To be sure, the ministers and the director general do have their informal conversations; and the director general is often inclined to yield to the wishes of the minister, for he knows that the minister has the king behind him and furthermore that in case of a serious conflict he may be dismissed, since the directors general belong as a rule to the class of civil servants who may be dismissed at discretion. But his yielding must always be cautious, for even when he gives way to the wishes of the minister he has to carry the responsibility himself. I know of very few cases where a conflict between the government and a director general has led to his being dismissed or removed, but several cases where there has been a permanent tension.

The central offices have yet another function. When the government has to decide a matter connected with the sphere of work belonging to a central office, it has to hear first the opinion of that office; our constitution provides in principle for such hearings. In such a case there is no doubt that the office should give its own opinion, even though it is quite incompatible with the policy of the government; the central office is expected to form its own judgment, based on its own experience. Such hearings are not only for the information of the government, but the riksdag also takes a great interest in them. When a royal proposition is brought before the riksdag it is expected to contain the opinions of the central offices concerned. The parliamentarians would not be satisfied if they did not have an opportunity to weigh the different opinions against one another. Many times the arguments of a central office have caused defeats in the riksdag for the government. In regard to other matters than government propositions submitted to the riksdag, one must remember the principle of the publicity of public documents. The reports of the central offices are, as a rule, public. They may be examined by the press and are very often published. Thus public opinion is regularly made familiar with the views of the central offices, and there is an unmistakable tendency to accept them as objective and unpolitical. To the minister who takes a divergent attitude this question is always put: how can you take the responsibility of going against the expert advice? Thus the administration is not only an acting body but also a thinking and willing organization with considerable moral force.

As for the local organs of state administration, many of them are subordinate to central offices, for example: the personnel of the state railways to the Railways Office, the customs officers to the Custom Office, and the schools to the School Board. All these people are used to regarding the director general, not the minister, as their proper head.

There are also local organs belonging to the state administration that are directly subordinate to the king in council. I mean especially the governors (*landshövdingar*), twenty-four in number. They are meant to be representatives of the king and have an old-fashioned title that may be translated as "king's commander." They are really, in a way, deputy kings in their provinces, keeping most wires of public administration in their hands and heading big administrative departments in their provinces. Their legal and real position is very much the same as that of the central offices.

One may wonder how it has been possible for the civil service and state administration to maintain their positions as somewhat independent powers in a system of balance. I have reminded you of the traditions, but how could they be maintained in face of victorious democracy? To understand the situation one must realize the weakness of government. At times when the king himself governed, an independent bureaucracy was thought to be a check upon monarchic omnipotence. And the parliamentary, or so-called parliamentary, governments of later times have until 1936 always or nearly always been supported only by minorities, the majorities therefore being pleased to see the power of a government they did not support but only tolerated limited by other elements. Now there is a new constitutional situation: Sweden has a government effectively supported by a majority. It remains to be seen whether the old constitutional principles will continue and whether the parliamentary majorities will take as great an interest as before in maintaining the traditional position of state administration and civil service. Many questions arise concerning the state administration. Will its unpolitical character be preserved? Will the legal status of civil servants remain unchanged? Will the ministers acquiesce, as they have done before, in having subordinates who do not conform to their wishes in everything? I may be allowed to say that I have a presentiment of coming changes, and I could relate facts that might give some ground for my suspicion. Of course, this is not meant as a criticism; it is probably inevitable that the establishment of new political forms should considerably affect the position of state administration.

THE old custom of having local affairs administered by the citizens themselves has never been abandoned in Sweden. There has always been a highly developed self-government in the cities. As for the rural districts, it was very important that the farming class maintained its personal freedom and the ownership of its lands so that the old hundred *things* could continue. The hundred *things* were, from the seventeenth century onward, presided over by a professional officer, but he was always surrounded by a permanent board of laymen, generally farmers. The hundred *things* had various affairs to administer. They drew up, for instance, the *cahiers* containing the grievances of the hundred, which their representatives used to present in the riksdag. But, more important, they had to see to the administration of law, which received through them, at any rate at the first stage, a popular character. The task of maintaining law and order was thought to depend not on learned lawyers alone, but on the broad mass of laymen, too.

Parish meetings, presided over by rectors, were another institution for popular self-rule. The parish residents came together to administer church discipline, to manage the business of the church, and also to consider a number of secular affairs such as poor-law administration and schools. Noblemen and their servants came together in the parish meetings with farmers, crofters, and farm-hands. Even in the palmy days of the class community the church asserted the principle of equality. One may ask if this is not only a beautiful fiction. I have pondered the question myself. A student who recently investigated this form of local government, especially in the eighteenth century, has shown however very conclusively that at least in some parts of the country all sorts of citizens were really active in the public affairs of parish meetings. He maintains that there was in this respect a difference between Sweden and England, where the vestry seems to have been more oligarchical. He is perhaps right in pronouncing the paradox that this wide participation was in part due to a weakness in the organization. In contradistinction to England, we had no rule about majority decisions; thus when general agreements were necessary everybody was expected to declare his position personally. Similar observations may be made about city government in earlier days.

Municipal government in Sweden has, then, old traditions. Modern legislation on this subject, from 1862 on, introduced no fundamental innovations; it simply made new constructions on an old basis, just as constitutional law today reflects the evolution of centuries.

Municipal government is now carried on in various incorporated units. We have provinces (*landstingsområden*), cities (*städer*), rural districts (*landskommuner*), and road districts (*vägdistrikt*). The rural districts cover the same areas as the old parishes (*församlingar*), which still exist as units for church, and sometimes school, affairs. To understand the functioning of the different forms of municipal units, it should be mentioned that the population of the provinces varies from 58,000 to 523,000 (average 218,000), the population of the cities from less than 1,000 to 557,000 (average 19,000), and the population of the rural districts from less than 100 to more than 25,000 (average 1,700). We have no experience of the problems that arise in great cities.

71

Municipal distribution is in a way very old-fashioned. Most of the rural districts coincide with parishes in existence since the Middle Ages, and only a fourth of our cities date from later times than the seventeenth century. It is therefore natural that a need for municipal readjustments should sometimes be felt. Special municipalities may be established for special purposes, and parts of one municipality may, even without its own consent, be transferred to another; in this way the natural development of big cities has been considerably facilitated. Sometimes a more thoroughgoing reorganization of municipal areas is urged, particularly in order to get rid of those very small municipalities that cannot without great difficulties organize satisfactory municipal governments. The deep-rooted feeling of solidarity that exists in most municipalities has, however, made such radical changes impossible.

The organization and the powers of municipalities in Sweden are regulated as a rule by statutes applicable to all municipalities belonging to a particular category. This principle does not prevent municipalities from deciding themselves to a certain degree, within the frame of the statutes, on matters of organization, nor does it mean that the state authorities which supervise municipalities (particularly the government and the governors) are not allowed in many cases to decide such questions. But a system of special statutes or charters regulating the position of different municipalities is entirely unknown to Swedish law. The riksdag does not meddle with the conditions of different municipalities.

In all municipalities the power belongs to councils elected proportionally by a popular vote (*landsting* in the provinces, *stadsfullmäktige* in the cities, *kommunalfullmäktige* in the rural districts). Only in small rural districts and in most parishes the citizens themselves assemble in town meetings to exercise the same powers as the councils do in other municipalities (*kommunalstämmor, kyrkostämmor*). The franchise regulations of 1862 gave an overwhelming influence to rich people, but since the reforms of 1907 and 1918 the franchise in municipal life has been the same as in the elections to the Second Chamber. Since that time, party organizations have taken the municipal as well as the national elections into their own hands. In most cases the elections are conducted on political lines. In most of the provinces, in most of the cities (among them the bigger ones), and in many other municipalities there is now a Socialist majority. The councils may be described as little municipal parliaments. Their supreme task is not to perform administrative work, but mainly to decide on the general policy of the municipalities. The number of the representatives is rather large in order to procure a comprehensive reflection of local opinion. The minimum number is fifteen; and in bigger municipalities it may be forty, fifty, or more. In this way a comparatively large number of citizens are brought to take part in municipal affairs and to feel civic responsibility.

What are the functions of the municipalities? What is their role in public administration? This question is to a certain degree left to be answered by the municipalities themselves. For they are, according to the municipal laws, entitled to take up any form of activity that may be said to fall within a very general clause: "common affairs of economy and public order." There would be good grounds for expecting that municipal activity, on this foundation, would develop along different lines in different places, and so it has to a certain degree. But a survey of municipal activity in Sweden does reveal some striking uniformities. All counties and all greater cities, for example, had spontaneously provided for public hospitals (of which we are very proud) before the statute of 1928 expressly provided for their doing so. Most cities have arranged for public utilities—gas, water, electricity, draining—and many of them have tried to regulate the supply of land by buying and selling real estate. There has been something of a common municipal standard, generally recognized, to which municipalities have had to conform even where no statutes required anything from them.

But this is not the whole truth. State legislation has also done much to make municipal work uniform. The state has, first, to a very great extent taken the municipalities into its service by charging them with the responsibility of providing for various public services. They had such duties of old under the poor law, the school laws, and the highway law. By later statutes they have been made responsible for providing for the police, for town-planning, for control over house building, for public health, for fire-brigades, for care of the sick, and above all for several sorts of social work, as for instance children's welfare. Sometimes the duties of municipalities are stated only in general terms, leaving to the discretion of municipal authorities how the duties should be fulfilled. But in many cases the statutes have gone far in deciding what the municipalities have to do. For instance the poor law indicates carefully when and in what ways poor people should be helped; and in organizing the public schools very little is left to municipal discretion. The provincial governors, poor-law supervisors, and state health officers, among others, exercise a very effective

74

state supervision of the municipal work done according to statutes, and in many fields state authorities may prescribe what shall be done in special cases, particularly when a municipality has failed to perform its duties.

Many functions of the municipalities are facilitated by grants-in-aid. There are general grants given to those municipalities whose tax rates have mounted very high owing to such expenses as those for poor relief and schools, which, according to the statutes, the municipalities have been obliged to pay. More important, however, are the grants given for special purposes like the salaries of teachers, nurses, and policemen, the running of certain hospitals, the construction and maintenance of highways, and housing. These grants are given primarily to equalize the burdens of such activities as are thought to be naturally municipal, but which would result in a great inequality of burdens should they fall completely on the municipalities, many of which are very small. The system of grants-in-aid has developed enormously in the last decades. This is largely a consequence of municipalities' being more and more subject to statutory requirements concerning their activity; such prescriptions would in many cases have been felt unfair had not the state at the same time helped the municipalities to perform their duties. In some fields a great percentage of the cost is paid by the state. This is the case, for instance, with the construction and maintenance of highways. Teachers' salaries also are practically borne by the state. The grants-in-aid are accompanied by an intensified state supervision and increased opportunities for state authorities to influence municipal policy.

In the presence of these developments different views are held. Some people think that municipal liberty is going to be limited too much by state control. It is also said that too much work and expense are required from the municipalities and that these difficulties cannot be overcome by grants from the state. The question has therefore been raised whether many municipal activities should not be handed over to the state. It is very characteristic, however, that as a rule the Swedish people shrink from taking such steps, although they have been taken in some cases. There is a deep-rooted feeling that the municipalities should have control, as far as possible, over local affairs.

The reason why this feeling still prevails is, of course, that in this way the citizens themselves are expected to take part in public administration. But is not this only a fiction? Do the citizens, the laymen, really take a decisive part in municipal government? To answer this question the structure of municipal organization should be considered.

Municipal administration is carried on by two elements. First, there are a great number of lay boards, instituted at the discretion of the municipal councils or prescribed by statute. In most cases when a statute requires something to be done it also provides for a municipal board to carry on the work: thus for instance there are poor relief boards, school boards, children's welfare boards, building boards, health boards, assessment boards, and others. In every municipality the statutes provide for a particular board to supervise municipal work as a whole, especially from a financial point of view. All these boards are entirely or for the most part elected by the municipal councils. Most often they are chosen on party lines. A proportional representation is, in many cases, prescribed by statute, and even when this is not the case a majority very seldom fills all posts on a board with its own political friends. The laymen who sit on them are expected to spend only a small part of their time on municipal work, and if they receive a compensation it is not very large. As a rule these lay boards conduct practically all municipal administration.

Secondly, there are, of course—especially in the cities, the provinces, and the road districts, but also in many rural districts—a large number of men and women who devote their efforts entirely to municipal work. They are ordinarily appointed by the boards—only in a few cases elected by the councils or by a popular vote—and they receive salaries. Their position may be compared to that of civil servants in state administration. Their legal status is not defined by statute, but as a rule their tenure is life-long, and it is exceptional for party standing to be considered in their selection. In some cases these officers act as board members, but usually they are subordinate to the boards and supposed to act according to their direction.

How has this system worked? Of course it is difficult, especially in the larger municipalities, to find people who are willing to sacrifice time and strength in the work of municipal boards. But up to now they have always been found; and should real difficulties arise we can in most cases fall back on the legal rule that everyone is obliged to assume such posts and can be punished if he does not fulfill his duties. The old idea that public service is a civic duty still survives in this rule. It is not so easy to make sure, however, that the members will have time to penetrate the questions put before them. The mass of work is sometimes overwhelming and the members are not always willing to spend hour after hour on tiresome details. Thus it happens, especially in large municipalities, that the real work of the boards consists only in confirming what their clerks have suggested. It also happens that civil servants really exercise a leadership. This is particularly true in the case of merely technical departments, but there are also examples of men who, though formally nothing but civil servants, from a practical point of view may be compared with American city managers.

Here we face a serious problem, which engages many people's minds in our municipalities. Some people are inclined to think that a great deal of the work would be better done if handed over to the professionals, or at any rate to people who may spend their whole time in the work, and that we had better accept this fact instead of conserving old-fashioned forms. A step in this direction has already been taken in Stockholm, where municipal leadership has been entrusted to six commissioners elected by the city council, without abolishing, however, the traditional board system.

On the whole we have felt that in spite of the difficulties, we can maintain the fundamental principle that elected citizens should not only deliberate and decide in the councils, which correspond to the riksdag in state life, but also carry on the administrative work as board members. Although laymen on the boards cannot do all we should like, nevertheless they do accomplish a great deal. The participation of laymen in municipal administration is a reality, not a fiction. The work done by the boards may be regarded as an important element in Swedish political life in several respects. There is in these boards as well as in the municipal councils a very profitable cooperation between men and women in different social positions and with different political views. It happens, of course, that a party majority sometimes carries on its policy ruthlessly, but often the work is pursued in good harmony, unpolitically, and objectively. Party politics do not play the same role in municipal as in national political life. Old traditions of self-government have perhaps contributed to maintain this state of affairs. It is also important, however, that the work that has to be done is to a great extent so carefully regulated by statute that there is not a very great margin for different political opinions. Thus, in municipal administration too, we have something of that unpolitical spirit, that spirit of objectivity, which prevails in state administration.

To carry on the municipal work the municipal councils are entitled to tax the inhabitants. This power is in some respects limited. First, its exercise supposes a regular budgeting. A budget should be passed every year, and taxation as a rule is allowed only for the actual needs provided for in the yearly budget. Second, the municipalities are not entitled to form tax systems at their pleasure. A municipal income tax statute gives in detail the rules according to which the citizens may be taxed; it decides for instance how far low incomes should be free from tax; it regulates the relation between the burdens of owners of real estate and other taxpayers; it prescribes that the municipal tax shall be proportional, whereas the state income tax is progressive. But the amount of taxation must be settled every year by the municipality itself; against excessive taxation there is only an indirect guarantee, that municipalities where taxation has reached a certain level are not allowed to undertake any new large expenditures without a two-thirds vote.

The liberty of action of the communities is also restricted as to borrowing. This always requires a two-thirds vote, and moreover in most cases the consent of the government is required. Governmental control of municipal finance, which has been exercised in this way, is thought to have been very fruitful. On the whole the financial status of Swedish municipalities seems rather satisfactory. Some of them to be sure have had difficulties, but I do not know of any case where a municipality has not been able to pay its debts.

How is it that municipal government does not degenerate, that the power does not fall into the hands of people who would use it for private or party purposes? Well, I do not pretend that abuses are lacking. I know of cases where a party majority has obviously favored its partisans. I know of private persons who have made a municipality serve their own economic interests in a way. I am anxious not to disseminate the false conception that our country is a utopia. We in Sweden also have to fight for honesty and integrity in municipal life.

Nevertheless our municipal standard is relatively good, largely because we have rather effective means of supervising municipal affairs. In some cases the decisions of municipal authorities are not valid without the consent of a state authority, i. e., the government or the governor. We also have the opportunity of suing before an administrative court, if a decision of a municipal organ is thought to be *ultra vires*, that is, beyond the powers granted to the municipality. If, for instance, a decision should be made on a matter that does not belong to the "common affairs of economy and public order" it may be invalidated. If a person thinks that a municipal board has not given him what he has a right to expect under the poor law or the building regulations, for example, then he has the same opportunity of suing them before a court. Municipalities are in this way subject to a very effective judicial supervision.

The importance of these checks on municipal arbitrariness and mistakes should not however be overemphasized. It is perhaps as important that there is among the citizens a rather wide-spread interest in good conduct of municipal affairs and that the citizens are inclined to react strenuously against wrong steps and misuse of power.

NEW DEVELOPMENTS IN PUBLIC
ADMINISTRATION

IN THE two preceding chapters I have surveyed the two traditional forms of public administration, both rooted in traditions of centuries. But new times and new needs have required new developments also. Public life is looking for new methods. We are living in a period of experiments and innovations. Since the time has not yet come to consolidate the new agencies and techniques it is a difficult task to survey them, but some tendencies can be discerned. There is, first, a growing habit of establishing new institutions outside of both state and municipal administration, institutions that are neither state nor municipal organs. Secondly, there is a tendency towards using in new forms the work of laymen, especially of laymen who may be said to represent the people or certain groups of citizens in some way. These tendencies may sometimes be observed as combined with each other; sometimes they appear separately.

For example there are several corporations that have been instituted for the sole purpose of giving more supple and businesslike organization to an activity that is in substance a state activity. We have, for instance, joint-stock companies owned by the state or under its control, which administer the tobacco monopoly and the wholesale liquor monopoly. There are other examples, but I think this phenomenon, which is, I believe, common to many countries, need not be stressed. There is more point in mentioning that activities which in many other countries are entrusted to separate corporations or carried on by private enterprise are in Sweden administered by ordinary state departments. For example, a state department manages the mighty forests of the state and sells their products. The state also runs railways and exploits water power for electrification.

As to laymen in state administration, it is quite natural that in several respects they should be found desirable. It must be remembered how markedly professional our civil service is. Very often it is felt that its work might be stimulated by laymen's ideas. Hence it is that in several boards and offices laymen with special technical knowledge cooperate with civil servants. Not only are the thoughts of laymen wanted; sometimes also their wills need to be considered. In many fields we find it desirable to let the influence of, for instance, the political parties or the interested social groups be felt.

The preparation of legislative and administrative reforms is usually entrusted to special investigating commissions (*kommittéer*) in which civil servants and technical experts cooperate with laymen. The collaboration established in such commissions between politicians from different parties (mostly members of the riksdag), lawyers, technicians, scientists, representatives of various social groups, and other laymen has often proved very fruitful. In the calm atmosphere of the *kommittéer* party prejudices can be subordinated to a common interest in reaching positive results. These commissions may in a way be regarded as a superstructure to the committee system of the riksdag, though they are always appointed by the government. It may be objected that this phenomenon has more to do with legislation than with administration. To be sure, the commissions are not administrative in function; they have only to draft, not to decide. Nevertheless they deserve to be mentioned in this connection, for they are playing an important role in planning administrative work. The riksdag is required by tradition to decide many questions of administrative organization, and just as commissions prepare other propositions laid before the riksdag by the king, they also prepare many proposals regarding administrative questions.

The popular will is, however, also displayed in state administrative work in its proper sense. A great number of special boards have been instituted in recent years, mainly in order to deprive the ordinary central offices of their influence over fields of administration that have seemed to be important or delicate from political or social points of view. Such boards have, for instance, been instituted to enforce or supervise the legislation concerning the normal working day, public accident insurance, unemployment policy, measures to support agriculture, and other measures. In such cases it has been thought convenient to call in people who represent more or less directly the great organizations of social groups—employers, laborers, and farmers. These have a very commanding position in economic life, especially the labor organizations. By this arrangement they also exercise a considerable influence over public administration. It goes without saying that those boards whose purpose is to express the popular will have a great deal of independence, although they are as a rule appointed by the government. In a sense the new arrangements have revived the old principle of administrative independence enjoyed by the central offices.

And now to a third phenomenon: the cases in which popular will and popular work are displayed outside state and municipal administration, where organizations of citizens are playing a role as separate bodies for the provision of public services. As a teacher of public law I am not a little confused in the face of these new devices. What we may establish is first, that an overwhelming multitude of associations have grown up in order to promote the interests of different social groups or to fulfill tasks of public interest. There is nothing in our law to impede their progress. Such associations have, secondly, been brought more and more into contact with state administration. The state may grant aids to them if they are working in the public interest; and as a consequence it may control them in one way or another, or entrust the fulfillment of special tasks to them. These are the facts; but how far are we entitled, in consequence of them, to regard these organizations as belonging to the public sphere of life, as taking part in public administration? I may be allowed to leave this question of legal classification out of account. It is difficult because we are now obviously in a state of transition, where new forms of organization are more and more being used for public purposes; such a dynamic time is not the time for lawyers to come with strict definitions.

Some few examples may elucidate the phenomenon I am speaking of. Considerable state grants are, for instance, given to many organizations for humanitarian, educational, and philanthropic purposes; to organizations for real estate credit; to health insurance organizations; and to organizations for voluntary training of military forces (the so-called *landstorm*). In every province there is an organization for agricultural economy that has to administer several sorts of state grants.

It is especially noteworthy that in recent years such organizations, which have to maintain special group interests, have even been thought fit for managing important public affairs. Thus, for instance, the administration of the unemployment insurance system, introduced in 1934, has been entrusted to labor unions; they have to manage it under a special statute, with grants from the state, and under its control. In the same way, cooperative organizations of agricultural producers carry out the new legislation that is intended to effect an agricultural adjustment. This development is caused by practical needs and by the commanding position that labor and agriculture have now in political and social life. It is not based on any political theory, but it means in reality that the old habit of self-government is finding new applications. We are, I think, justified in maintaining that the flora of free associations, which has grown so rich and so multifarious, has been fed in the fertile soil of local government traditions. With the extension of state activity we have come to the point where these popular associations begin to assume functions within public administration. Alongside of the deep-rooted local self-government there is use for a self-government of classes and other social groups.

The present state of affairs is, as I have just pointed out, a state of transition, and nobody can judge at this moment how far our public administration may develop in the direction I have indicated. The development has, however, gone far enough to allow us to see the new problems it must raise. Can we hope to find in the interests-groups that become occupied in public administration the public spirit that has been displayed in municipal administration? And what is to be done to secure a harmony between the special interests of the organizations and the public interests entrusted to them? Some years ago it was a great political question whether there could be found some way of regulating the exercise of power of the mighty economic organizations and for preventing their undue interference in economic life and with the liberty of the citizen. This question has been put aside since the great victory of the Socialists in the elections of 1936. But I am sure that such questions cannot be escaped in the end, especially if the accruement of political functions to the economic activities of these essentially private organizations continues.

THE ACTIVE CITIZEN

To UNDERSTAND the political and social life of a foreign country one should consider above all what the state is to its citizens. One does not catch the spirit of a people by studying only the organization and functions of different political and administrative entities, nor is it enough to study social and economic conditions. One must also regard the citizen in his relation to the state—how he is influencing the life of the state and how the state is influencing him.

Government and citizen! One needs to consider all sorts of citizens, rich and poor, powerful and weak, those who take a warm interest in public affairs and those who do not care for them at all. One should avoid empty abstractions. We have learned in political science and public law that the average citizen with whom legislators and political thinkers occupied themselves in earlier times was a pure phantom. We have to deal with citizens of very different sorts. Something must be said, therefore, about the social structure of Sweden.

If you consult members of the Swedish population in the United States you may be told that the immigrants came from a country imbued with class discriminations and prejudices to a community where liberty and equality prevailed. Well, it is a fact that class distinctions have played a great role in Sweden, not only in social but also in political life. Until 1865 the organization of our parliament was based on them. It was quite natural too that the farmers deeply resented their position as the lowest of the four

estates. In the sixties a new political system was established, but instead of the old class distinctions it had distinctly plutocratic features, especially in municipal life.
Nowadays however there is nothing left of the privilege
system of earlier days. Of course if you visit Sweden you
may possibly be struck by manners that seem to indicate
such differences. In our way of living we may have retained
some habits and forms originating in a society with class
distinctions, a society where the royal court, nobility, and
bureaucracy held strong positions in men's minds. But it
must be emphasized that these forms, if there are such, do
not imply legal inequality. As to social and economic inequality, I feel sure that they do not go so deep as in many
other countries. We have relatively few people of great
wealth, and not very much of the greatest depths of
wretchedness. It is also of no little importance that the
Swedish people are very homogeneous from an ethnologi-
cal point of view. We know nothing about racial contrasts.

And now to consider the ways in which Swedish citizens
are influencing government. I may start by summing up
some facts that have already been mentioned in other
connections.

The Swedish people were always politically active to a
remarkable degree. Even in those centuries when in most
countries public power was concentrated in the hands of an
absolute monarch and a bureaucracy entirely dependent
on him, the Swedish people had to take a more or less
active and responsible part in public affairs, in parliament,
in municipal government, and in the courts of law. I do not
wish to idealize the situation; it is important to point out
that in Sweden as in other countries political power certainly has often been misused for private purposes. But

self-government, in the state and municipalities, exercised for centuries, could not fail to foster at the same time valuable moral convictions, habits, and traditions. Sweden was a school of self-government, where the people were educated to look upon the state and the municipalities neither as foreign, hostile powers nor as instruments for promoting their own interests, but as a common concern, for which they had to share the responsibility. Public affairs were in this way made familiar to the Swedish people. What German authors have called the active or political status became, through the educative work of generation after generation, a natural ingredient in man's life.

To survey civic influence in our political life of today we have to consider in what ways laymen take part in public affairs. In passing it should be observed, however, that according to Swedish traditions the professional work of a civil servant is regarded, more than in many other countries, as something of a civic contribution. With his relative independence and with his responsibility not only to his superiors but also to the courts and to the general public he is, even in his public work, something of a free citizen.

The average citizen takes his part in public affairs as a voter. Every second year he is called to the polls for elections either to the Second Chamber or to the municipal councils; in small municipalities he may also take part in the town meetings. He takes very little part, however, in electing other officers than the representatives. There is a decidedly "short ballot" in Sweden. The administrative officers of the state and the municipalities are generally not elected by a popular vote. There are only a few exceptions to this rule: parish rectors and some other clergymen are most often elected by the parish residents, but in many cases they are appointed by the government; in small municipalities teachers are also elected by a popular vote; finally, the presidents (*borgmästare*) of the city courts (*rådhusrätter*) are appointed by the government from lists of three candidates proposed through a popular vote. In all these cases the elections are made for life. One other exception should be emphasized: our law courts of first instance in the country districts (*häradsrätter*) still consist of one lawyer, as president, and twelve laymen elected by a popular vote for a term of six years.

The referendum plays a very unimportant role. It is unknown in the municipalities. In state politics the people may be consulted by a referendum, and were consulted once, in 1922, on the question of introducing prohibition. But it is constitutionally impossible to leave a question to be *decided* by a referendum. To be sure, the general elections of today often decide certain actual reform issues; in this way the importance of the electorate, in its electing function, has increased in some measure at the expense of the riksdag.

If the citizens in general are not called to take so great a part in public affairs as is the case in the United States, it may perhaps be said on the other hand that laymen, whether elected or appointed, play a considerable part in legislative, administrative, and judicial functions. They act as members of the riksdag, as members of the municipal councils and boards, as members of the *häradsrätter*, and in many posts belonging to state administration. Thus in various ways the will and the thought of the public are represented in public work, not by people who make the public service a full-time job, but by people who spend only a part of their time in working for the public. A considerable percentage of Swedish citizens are thus made familiar with public affairs. They learn to regard them from other standpoints than those of individuals, and to feel, more or less, a public responsibility.

It may be asked, however, whether in these ways popular will and popular thought are really represented. We should, of course, be well aware of all those circumstances that may make the representatives differ from those represented, and those circumstances, too, that may make the representatives mere decorations, tools in the hands of other wills. As to the riksdag, it has already been mentioned that it gives, from a social point of view, a fairly true picture of the people as a whole. What is true of the riksdag is still more true of municipal life.

Then there is the second question: are the laymen who take part in public work really able to assert their own opinions? To be sure, their tasks are sometimes so great that they must often be overwhelmed by the opinions and the wills of experts and professionals. So it is in the riksdag, in municipal life, and in the courts; but laymen are still far from mere tools. I may take the work in the *häradsrätter* as an example. The laymen in these courts are certainly not able to display popular sentiments as imperatively as an Anglo-Saxon jury. They do not have at all the same power as these juries, for they can overrule the president only if they are all united against him. But their position is fairly strong, inasmuch as they do not come in for special cases but are elected to sit in the court for years, and inasmuch also as they take part in all the work of the court. Most lawyers who have worked in such courts will tell you how fruitful the discussions between lawyers and laymen are, and testify to the value of the common sense and knowledge of life that the laymen bring with them. We are happy that our law has always been administered under such a fertile collaboration of skilled lawyers and experienced laymen, who will become, in their permanent work at the courts, familiar with law, imbued with legal ways of thinking, and able to express a popular sense of justice. Similar observations may be made about the riksdag, with its deep-rooted tendency to judge independently the questions that come before it, and the municipal boards.

The question of the influence of the citizens upon public activity is not, however, exhausted by telling in what ways they act as organs of the state and of municipalities. They may also exercise such an influence in other ways. They may work from the outside, for private interests or to promote such public interests as they believe in. They may work as organized groups or as individuals. They may use the methods of persuasion or of pressure, and to exercise pressure various means may be used—money for instance. They may use these methods against the voters, in order to have people that they trust elected, or against the representatives and the civil service.

It is difficult to state to what extent influence is exerted in these ways, but I venture to maintain a few theses. Public opinion in its unorganized forms, expressed for instance by the newspapers, is certainly of great importance, and its influence is strengthened by the publicity that makes it possible for the general public to get information about the work going on in the administration and to judge it with a certain amount of knowledge of the subjects. I do not think, on the other hand, that we have very much organized collective influence, either by persuasion or by pressure. The Swedish people are not, I believe, organized to such an extent as Americans, or at any rate they are not organized in such a way as to affect government. Parties are certainly important elements in Swedish political life, but they do not work at all as agencies to promote the private interests of their partisans. Of course their representatives, in municipal councils for instance, may seek to help their fellow-partisans; but the party itself is not an instrument for such work. Furthermore, although some organizations try to influence government in one way or another, they do so mainly by addressing themselves to the cabinet, to the riksdag, and to municipal councils. That is to say, they work publicly, by arguments that may be known to the public and must stand against public criticism. Of course I am not so naive as to believe that there are not also secret ways that cannot always be observed. But the methods that are used to establish popular control in public affairs must render such secret influences rather difficult.

This is in harmony with a fact I should like finally to emphasize. It is a general belief that we have been spared the worst forms of undue influence exerted by money. To be sure, it is difficult to discover the ways in which such an influence is exerted, and still more difficult to decide in what cases such influence should be characterized as undue. I do not doubt that people who have money at their disposal are sometimes able to procure advantages for themselves and their friends that other people could not obtain. While thus admitting many exceptions, I must, however, confess that I think the general confidence in the honesty of our representatives, our civil service, and our municipal administration is on the whole well founded. It is difficult to buy advantages, and the influence of capital, in its totality, is not easily exercised otherwise than by persuasion.

It may be concluded that the influence of citizens on government is exercised mainly by their filling responsible public positions, and less by their working from without to put pressure on government in support of private interests.

CONSTRAINT AND LIBERTY

HAVING considered how the citizens influence public life, we turn to the question how the state and the municipalities affect private life. They do so in the first place by imposing restrictions on liberty, in the second place by helping the citizens in one way or another. I shall treat each of these phases separately. Thus my first question refers to the ways in which the state limits the freedom of the citizens. I have to survey the citizens' so-called passive status, in which they are subject to the prescriptions of the state, and their so-called independent status, in which they are free.

The constitutional starting point of this survey has already been given. There are, with one exception, no constitutional provisions limiting state activity or safeguarding a sphere of civic liberty. Thus the liberty of citizens is at the discretion of the legislative power. But are questions of civic liberties really reserved exclusively for the riksdag? Modern experiences with delegated legislation lead us to put this question. It will be remembered that the king—that is, the government—is entitled by provisions of the constitution to legislate on different matters, even infringing upon the liberty of citizens. Our constitutional law does not prescribe, as in so many other countries, that such infringements shall not be made without the consent of the representatives. This right of the king is, however, at present not far from being a dead letter. Legislative powers are, indeed, often delegated to the king or to administrative departments by acts of the riksdag, but in such cases the riksdag has been careful to circumscribe rather scrupulously the powers delegated insofar as civic rights are concerned. Only during the war were any considerable deviations made from this principle. Thus most steps taken to curtail civil liberty are made by statute, with that possibility of public discussion which is connected with legislative procedure.

The enforcement of statutes that imply a limitation of liberty depends mainly on the administrative organs of the state: the king in council, the central offices, the governors, and so on. According to Anglo-Saxon terminology these powers would certainly in many cases be called semi-judicial.* The question how far the administrative departments should be allowed to make such decisions does not, however, as in the Anglo-Saxon countries, represent any grave political or constitutional problem. They had such functions of old; and, considering the characteristic structure of the departments and their legalistic traditions, the rights of the citizens have never been felt to be seriously threatened by administrative discretion. Constitutional principles as to the separation of powers cannot be adduced against entrusting such powers to administrative departments. In some instances, however, a sort of safeguard against administrative arbitrariness has been established by entrusting important functions to boards composed wholly or partly of laymen. Several types of municipal boards have been used for this purpose, such as for instance building boards, to regulate the erection and alteration of

---

*On the other hand, administrative authorities are entrusted to make decisions in disputes between private citizens or corporations only in exceptional cases. In ancient times administrative bodies had such powers in many cases, but during the nineteenth century the principle was established that all such cases should go to the general courts of law. In this respect the powers of our administrative departments do not go so far as the powers of certain administrative authorities or tribunals in the United States.

buildings in the cities; health boards, to take measures in the interest of public health; children's welfare boards, to separate vicious and neglected children from their parents; and temperance boards, to take care of alcoholics. The confidence put in the administrative organs of state is, however, clearly illustrated by the fact that in all these cases the provincial governor has a check on municipal activity. In some cases the decisions of the board have to be confirmed by him, in other cases he may reverse them after appeal. Income tax assessment is entrusted to municipal boards that act under the control of administrative courts.

The intervention of the courts is very seldom required to authorize a measure taken against an individual in the common interest. They have power, in principle, to decide civil and criminal cases, but not when the question at issue is what a private person owes to the state. Only in rare instances does an administrative authority have to ask for the help of a court of law to have a measure enforced.

To consider the different aspects of liberty, I may begin with property. Sweden is, and was always, a non-socialist community. Although property is not placed under constitutional guarantees, it is nevertheless, and always has been, respected. As in other countries, one cannot be deprived of one's property without due compensation. This is the principle of the expropriation legislation and of many other statutes that require the citizen to give up his property for a common purpose. The most important question however is this: how far is the citizen subject to regulations as to the use of his property? Swedish law has developed many restrictions of this sort that would perhaps in the United States be regarded as contradictions to the proprietor's rights. Such restrictions may be more natural in an old country than in a comparatively young one; Swedish proprietors have been accustomed to them from ancient times. The freeholders were not completely free; among the inhabitants of a village there was a ramified network of mutual dependence, preventing the proprietor from using his land as he liked. There was also a complicated system of regulations in the interest of the community. These were supported by a theory of the dominion of the Crown over the land, and aimed at preserving the value of the real estate in order that there might be a secure foundation for national economic life and national finances. Of course the nineteenth century relaxed these ties, but when, at the end of that century, the demands for a public control over the use of real estate became urgent for new reasons, such control did not appear too foreign to our traditions and our ideas of justice.

Thus there have been no great difficulties in establishing several limitations of the proprietor's rights. We have, for instance, far-reaching regulations on the conservation of forests, which are of a very great importance in our economy, and the exploitation of water power and of minerals. The subdivision of real estate is placed under public control. To keep the land in the hands of the farming class, joint-stock companies are not as a rule allowed to buy real estate in the rural districts. The town planning statute, the building regulations, and the health regulations form a considerable check on the chances of proprietors, in the rural districts as well as in the cities, to exploit their real estate.

Similar observations may be made as to the regulation of industry. There was in earlier times—let us say a hundred years ago—no liberty of industry in Sweden. On the contrary, industry was placed under rather efficient public control, according to the ideas of mercantilism. To be sure, other ideas prevailed at the middle and at the end of the nineteenth century, but when the inconveniences of an unlimited freedom became apparent, the demands for regulation could, on this point too, appeal to old traditions. The legislation to preserve workingmen from the dangers of industrial labor commenced as early as the eighties; it revived in some ways the still living traditions of handicraft guilds. This legislation has later developed to a high degree of efficiency. There was in Sweden no need for industrial codes to ameliorate the position of the workingmen. The eight-hour day law (1919) was a natural continuation of this legislation. This year (1938) a law was passed securing for workingmen some vacation every year.

In other ways also economic life has been put under public control. Banking and insurance are very closely controlled. A great many occupations require public authorization, at first only to prevent such dangers as might arise out of certain forms of industry, such as electrical works, but later also in order to procure a good organization of the economic forces of the country. The professional motor traffic, for instance, is subject to a very effective regulation. The agricultural crisis in the thirties has considerably augmented these forms of state intervention, and agricultural production has in many forms been put under public control.

Thus in many ways the state has come to control the economic forces of the country. There are, moreover, other fields where the freedom of the citizens has been considerably restricted. Some few examples may be mentioned. The Children's Welfare Act considerably restricts parental authority; with the consent of the governor, a municipal children's welfare board is entitled to separate children from their parents if they are depraved or if their home is in such a state that there is a risk of their becoming depraved. In such cases the public takes over the responsibility for their being brought up to become good citizens. The state also takes care of grown-ups. Among the work done to maintain good public morals, I may especially mention our temperance legislation. We have not, like our neighboring countries, Norway and Finland, tried a prohibition policy; but the consumption of liquors in restaurants is regulated in several ways, and there is the fundamental principle that a citizen may not buy spirits at his own discretion in liquor shops. As a rule one is not entitled to buy more than four liters a month, and if a person is likely to abuse spirits a lower maximum may be established for him. This so-called individual control, introduced about twenty years ago, has of course aroused a great deal of dissatisfaction, and there have been many complaints of its being arbitrarily handled. To many people it has seemed to be a most formidable encroachment upon private liberty, but there is no doubt that it has helped very much to improve public morals. I believe that the control is not felt as a very severe drag upon a reasonable consumption of liquors, and it has spared us the difficulties of prohibition.

Turning now to the liberty of thought and opinion, I may begin with an historical observation. It should be emphasized that in ancient times Swedish liberty did not at all comprise a complete freedom of thought. On the contrary, a certain common standard of thought was rigorously maintained, insofar as everybody had to believe in the creed of the established church. This alliance between church and state was consummated in the sixteenth and the seventeenth centuries, particularly at the time of the fight against the Counter Reformation. The common faith was in those days an integrating power of immense importance. It was felt, with something of the same intensity as in modern dictatorships, that a national unity requires a basis of common moral and human ideals. Comparative studies have made it clear that in very few countries was religious unity maintained as strictly as in Sweden. Many of the Swedish emigrants to the United States had felt the heavy pressure of the church against the dissenting religious movements that developed in the nineteenth century. Such experience helped very much to maintain, among the Swedish population in America, the feeling that the people in the country they had left lived in oppression and bondage.

The old system had to fall, however, in the middle of the nineteenth century. We still have, to be sure, a state church, of which everybody who has not formally left it to enter some free church is legally a member. But anyone may do so if he wishes, and if one remains in the state church one does not feel any ties originating in this membership. There are several free churches, most of which arose under an obviously Anglo-Saxon influence. They have played a considerable role in maintaining and developing a free and active citizenship and have fostered an interest in public activity and a practice of free collaboration that were valuable elements in the formation of both the Liberal and the Socialist parties. Many people, too, do not care for any church at all; the idea that everyone should be an active church member is far from being as common as in the United States.

What, then, about public opinion on other questions? Legislation has left a nearly unlimited sphere for public discussion, for the propagation of different political, moral, and social opinions. This principle was not maintained only by the liberalism of the nineteenth century; it is still upheld. Modern tendencies towards limiting economic freedom have no counterpart in the field of freedom of thought or in fields connected therewith. There is a nearly unlimited right of public meetings. The right of association is also practically unlimited. It might, of course, in the case of workingmen and other employees, be restricted by the employers, by their refusing to recognize organizations for collective bargaining or even by their prohibiting employees from joining the organizations. As a matter of fact labor unions have had to fight for their existence, but for many years no industrial employer has been able to persist in such a policy against his workers. Nowadays the rights of white-collar employees and of agricultural laborers are also commonly recognized. Even civil servants are allowed not only to form associations but also to negotiate with the state authorities about their rights.

The best illustration of the attitude of Swedish law toward freedom of thought may perhaps be found in our legislation on the liberty of the press. It is a striking fact that one of our constitutional laws from the beginning of the nineteenth century regulates this topic in detail. As a matter of fact, we had our first constitutional law on the liberty of the press as early as 1766. Because in other respects we have not been at all anxious to safeguard individual rights by constitutional provisions, this is a very remarkable exception, and a rather significant one. Our constitutional fathers did not place economic rights under constitutional guarantees, but they did secure the freedom of minds. This was not because they thought this freedom one of the inalienable rights of the citizens but because they believed that free public discussion and a well informed public opinion were integrating powers in political life. This idealistic creed was typical of optimistic liberalism (though it originated in Sweden before the liberal era), but it has been subsequently maintained. It is not possible in any way to interfere with productions of the press. Only if the freedom is abused in certain ways, exactly described in the constitutional law, may the author be punished; and in these cases we have a jury system that is, in practice, very indulgent towards offenders. It rarely happens that an author is punished.

In a word, all sorts of opinions are left practically free, to persuade the public as far as they can. Even in a grave crisis or in a war it would be legally impossible to restrict the fundamental freedom of the press except by altering the constitutional law.

The standpoint Swedish law has taken presupposes that freedom of thought will not give rise to convictions so strong, so opposed to each other, and so hostile to the legal order that the foundations of social life will be imperiled. Remembering the experiences of many other countries of today, we must, however, ask whether this assumption has been justified. Has a sufficient amount of solidarity been maintained in the economic, social, and political struggles? Certainly we have had to reflect upon the problem. We have seen situations where ideas of labor solidarity, with about half of the people behind them, have come into rather frightening conflict with views maintained as eagerly by others. In such cases there has been reason for asking whether there are common fundamental conceptions of law and justice. We have groups, also, that speak of other methods than persuasion in political struggle, and perhaps also think of using them: Nazis and Communists. They have recently (1933) led the riksdag to take some measures limiting, very slightly, the freedom of association.

But if there are some grounds for fear, there are also grounds for hope that the fissures produced in our national unity by the uncontrolled spread of differing thoughts will not go too far or too deep. The sense of national unity must be rather strongly anchored in men's minds when it rests on centuries of free cooperation. The relative homogeneity of the Swedish people is also of some importance. We have been spared those concussions that are the consequence of grave crises and wars. There is, for instance, no class that has been, like the German middle class, brought to despair by economic disaster. As to the workers, their situation has been constantly improved, owing to increasing general prosperity and to social legislation. The boundary between the middle and lower classes has become more and more obscure; in wide spheres of labor a middle-class consciousness is developing. And it is not without importance that the Labor party has now a commanding position in state and municipal politics. In this situation there are chances for smoothing out those bitter sentiments caused by the proletariat's feeling of being exploited. We are now living and making our policy in a spirit of mutual confidence and understanding and respect, many differences existent in earlier times having been forgotten.

Thus thoughts and opinions have free play without any real danger of disintegrating or even threatening seriously the moral foundations of state life. But I think we should be aware that we owe this position to extraordinarily favorable circumstances: the strength of our national economy just now, and the absence of grave international difficulties. The general feeling of satisfaction is due to all that the state has been able to do for its citizens under these good conditions. Should the foundations of our national welfare be seriously attacked—and this may easily happen in a new world crisis—we may have to reckon with an outburst of contrary feelings and aspirations. We could not say whether in such a situation, of which Sweden has had no experience for a very long time, our traditional liberalism could be maintained without serious damage.

The discussion of civic liberty should not be finished without considering another aspect of the question, which has not yet been touched upon. We have to consider not only the encroachments upon liberty from the state's side, but also from other sides. Under a liberal government there is, as everyone knows, always a chance for powerful private forces to get, by persuasion or by economic pressure, that hold on men which the state refrains from claiming. It has always been so, but only in the last decade have we come to realize the problem. There are the well-known monopolistic tendencies in industry. There is the influence of the labor organization, which has today a really very strong position in Sweden. Its influence is exercised with success in many different directions, against its members, against people who are expected to join the organizations but refuse to do so, against people who wish to work in a profession but are not accepted by the trade-union concerned, and against people who in other ways oppose or obstruct the policy of the organization. The owners of industry are organized in the same way, in a great organization comprising nearly all producers of any importance; its methods are in many respects similar to those of the labor organization. In the last five years agriculture, which was earlier extremely individualistic, has also developed a powerful system of cooperative associations, encouraged in many ways by the state. These have grown up very rapidly and now claim from the farmers the same sort of loyalty and concord that the labor organization has so successfully established within the working class.

The methods that all these organizations use in their fights have, of course, in many circles aroused a great deal of dissatisfaction. People who are for some reason in opposition to them and exposed to their pressure have come to feel that they endanger the old Swedish freedom. One of the dominating issues of Swedish policy in the first half of the thirties was the question of legislation to regulate in some way the methods of economic struggle. A very interesting legislative problem, indeed; but it proved difficult. There was a strong feeling for the necessity of equality; therefore no sort of organization should be discriminated against. It was not the intention to make special rules for labor organizations, producers' organizations, and so on, but to find rules that could be adapted to all sorts of organizations. When the question was put in this way, however, there developed, against all rules proposed, a strong opposition from organizations of different sorts that were anxious to retain their liberty. Of decisive importance was the opposition from labor and agriculture, which are now in possession of the political power. For the present the question has been consigned to oblivion. The organizations are, so to say, accepted, along with their methods of opposition and coercion.

THE SERVICE-STATE

I HAVE spoken of the Swedish citizen both as subject to the commands of the state and the municipalities and in his sphere of liberty. It remains to consider what the state and the municipalities do for him. I am, then, going to present to you a species of the modern service-state. When doing so I shall try, of course, to confine myself to such phenomena as I believe to be, in one way or another, characteristic of our political life.

To promote the economic development of the country the state has taken important enterprises into its hands instead of leaving them to private undertaking, especially in the field of communications. In our expansive country, with its rather sparse population, it was always the business of government to provide as good communication as possible. The maintenance of highways in particular was important, and the significance of the highways has, of course, increased enormously in the last decades. The task always was and still is fulfilled by a special class of municipalities acting under state control: the road districts. In recent times the state has spent many hundred million crowns (this is a great deal of money in my country) to improve the highways. These works have played a great role in our unemployment policy.

When the question of building railways was up for decision in Sweden in the middle of the nineteenth century, it was, in consideration of these traditions, quite natural that the state should take charge of this function too. The main railways were built and run by the state itself; and so they are still. In other cases the operation of railways was, by concessions, left to private enterprise, but these railways were from the beginning put under effective state control. Many of them were, as a matter of fact, municipal enterprises, the municipalities being to a great extent shareholders in the railway companies. Moreover, according to the concessions, the state always has a right to take over private railways upon payment of an indemnity. In recent times the state has in one way or another acquired a good many of them. Just now the question is being considered whether the state should on a large scale take over railways still owned by private corporations or in some way promote their organization into more comprehensive systems.

As the state has run the railways, so it has also run other utilities, telegraph and telephone for instance. In earlier days there were private telephone companies too, but nowadays the state has in fact, if not legally, a monopoly. Radio broadcasting is operated by one semiofficial corporation. The waterfall administration is another vast state enterprise; a very great part of the electrical energy in Sweden is produced by this state department.

Like the state, the municipalities also are running great enterprises to provide public service. In most cities and many other municipalities electricity is distributed by the municipalities themselves. Many cities have gas works, and some are running tramways and autobus lines. Everywhere the water and draining services are municipal enterprises.

Public opinion is, as far as I know, satisfied with this state of affairs. You may call it a sort of socialism. But it has nothing to do with socialist theories. It was always thought quite natural that the state and municipalities should provide for utilities that are as essential as those I have mentioned. I am no economist, and I cannot judge whether the services have been, in public hands, cheaper or more expensive for the citizens than would have been the case had they been left to private activity. At any rate business in the hands of the state and municipalities can be better controlled by the public, and this is an advantage we appreciate.

There has been more dissension on another form of public activity. To promote temperance the liquor traffic has been, first by measures of the municipalities and then by general legislation (1917), reserved for a special sort of joint-stock companies, which are, as a matter of fact, only a disguise for state activity. Thus the greed of private gain cannot work to an increase of liquor consumption, the whole of the profit coming into the public treasury. This arrangement has been criticized by those who are displeased because the state is making liquor too expensive as well as by those who object that the state has a financial interest in an increase of the liquor traffic. But I can safely assert that a great majority of citizens do not object to getting their spirits from the public, just as they get water, gas, electricity, radio, and telephones. We have grown accustomed to a tobacco monopoly (1914), too, but the interest taken by the Socialist party in establishing new forms of state monopolies—a coffee monopoly, a gasoline monopoly—has aroused a great deal of concern and opposition.

Another vast field of public activity is medical service. To be sure, there are private hospitals, but not many. The great majority of hospitals in Sweden, beyond question, are in the hands of the provinces and the large cities. They are obliged to provide hospitals according to the actual need in different parts of the realm. The fees are far below cost; only in a few cases do they exceed two *kronor* (fifty cents) a day (for a private room the fees are higher, of course, ranging from eight to twelve *kronor* a day). The care provided is on a level with the best standards of Swedish medical science. Lunatic asylums are run by the state; here too we have established the principle that there should be a place for everyone who has need of being taken care of. There are special institutions, too, for imbeciles, the disabled, the blind, and so on, established by the state or the municipalities. The state and the cities also pay a great number of doctors to supervise, each in his own district, the people's health and to give medical attention. In many ways they are assisted by district nurses paid by the state and the provinces. Just now we are planning a comprehensive system of dental hygiene. In a word, the great mass of Swedish citizens are accustomed to expect medical attendance from the public, not from private doctors and hospitals, and to expect it at very moderate prices if not gratuitously.

And so it is with education. All education was in the beginning thought to be a church affair—but it should be remembered that the established church of Sweden was in principle identical with the state, or with the people. Thus the traditional church activities have not, as in the United States, been maintained by a great number of churches and religious organizations, all working on a voluntary basis and appealing, with moral and religious arguments, to the social consciousness and the benevolence of those who are able to help. It was quite natural that the educational tasks of the church should pass over almost imperceptibly from the church to the state and to the municipalities under state control. The elementary (public) schools are in the hands of the municipalities, but have been put under a gradually intensified supervision in connection with increasing grants-in-aid. Nowadays the standard of elementary education is very carefully settled by state legislation, leaving only details to be arranged at municipal discretion. Practically every child in Sweden attends an elementary school till his eleventh year, and the majority remain until their thirteenth or fourteenth year. Most of the secondary (high) schools are state schools; there are only a few private schools. It has always been regarded as a public task to provide this sort of education, and to facilitate the attendance of poor people, the schools always have been very cheap. I think it has been of great importance to the spirit of our people that during this decisive age in human development young people from the most different social classes have always had to work together and to be exposed to the same sort of influences, to be imbued with the same knowledge and the same sets of general ideas. Just as the state has its secondary schools, it also has universities. To be sure, there are private universities too, but they form, in some way, together with the state universities, only a link in a single educational system. To put their examinations on a par with those of the state universities, private universities have had to maintain the same standard and to conform in many respects to state regulations.

You see that a Swedish citizen is to a notable extent dependent on the state. There is no choice for him. He has to accept what the state offers as to public utilities, liquors, medical assistance, education. The state has in this way powerful instruments to influence private life. If we accept this state of affairs it is because we have not seen much of the inconveniences of state activity. Our educational system, for instance, is not at the service of one theory of life; it gives reasonable room for different opinions; and on the whole, the public arrangements have not interfered too strongly in those spheres of life where most people prefer to choose their own way. It is possible, nevertheless, that the question how far the state should go in this respect will very soon be a leading political issue. Many people, especially some doctors, economists, and politicians belonging to the Labor party, would like to go very far in state arrangements for promoting public health. There is a tendency toward rational planning for housing, nourishment, education, and so on. I wonder if some people are not overestimating the capacity of the state for arranging private life rationally and lifting responsibilities from its citizens.

In most of the services I have dealt with there is a social purpose. But the aim of leveling economic differences is still more apparent in other forms of public activity, where the state or the municipalities are giving aid in one way or another to people in distress. The basis of all this work is the relief to the poor. It developed in somewhat the same way as elementary education: in the beginning it was a religious duty, and the work was organized by the municipalities under the leadership of the clergy. It is still a municipal task. But the church management has disappeared, and the state has been led more and more to direct the work, the poor law defining carefully what the municipalities have to do. Municipal authorities have, however, to judge the need of the applicant, and decide in what way the help should be given. Thus, though the citizen has, in principle, a right to be helped, he is in a somewhat humiliating position when he asks for it.

The poor law has, however, in this century been comple-
mented by a long series of statutes improving the position
of people in distress. It is common for them all to define
more exactly the situations in which help should be given
and what help can be claimed, so that the citizen has well
defined rights to assert. First came the accident insurance
acts of 1901 and 1916, giving everybody who is working
for another person, whether in industry or at home, a
stipulated compensation if he is injured by accident in his
work or in connection therewith. These acts are supple-
mented by later acts, procuring a similar indemnification
in the case of occupational diseases. The costs are paid by
the employers, who are charged with the insurance pre-
miums. A comprehensive system of public pensions was
introduced in 1913. At the age of 67 every citizen has a
right to a small pension, provided he has paid the fees required, and so has everybody who becomes disabled before
that age. If the pensioner is poor, he may receive a considerable increase, varying according to his economic position and the costs of living. It would serve no purpose to
give figures, but I should state that the pensions, which
were considerably enhanced in 1935 and 1937, are considered large enough to procure a scanty living. The citizen
has in this way what may be called a legal right to security
in his old age. We all know however that it will be a very
heavy task for the taxpayers to meet these liabilities in an
age of a sinking birth-rate and increasing duration of life.
The pensions legislation has been amplified recently by
several forms of pecuniary assistance: to blind people, to
orphans, to children one of whose parents is dead or disabled, to confined women. Health insurance organizations
receive considerable grants from the state; they are open to

everybody. During the World War and after it (till 1923 and in 1931–35) the unemployment question was of great importance. Sweden has tried to solve the problem mainly by arranging several sorts of public works, but pecuniary assistance has also been given on a large scale by the state and by many municipalities. Since 1934 the state has given grants to unemployment insurance associations, especially those established by trade-unions. In recent years state and municipalities have given large subventions and loans to counteract the scarcity of housing.

Social assistance is altogether organized by statutes. In some cases the state pays all the costs; in others the municipalities are taken into the service of the state, being obliged to contribute in one way or another. Are, then, the municipalities allowed to give aid in other forms or to give amounts supplementary to the assistance prescribed by statute? This is, as a matter of fact, a very important question, for in many municipalities the majorities are inclined to improve the position of the poor classes at the expense of the taxpayers. Thus, for instance, in Socialist municipalities there was in the times of unemployment a tendency to follow a very generous policy. Now the municipalities may give such additional assistance to a certain extent, according to special statutes, but as a general rule the right of self-government does not comprise the right to give pecuniary assistance without special statutory authorization. It is the business of government and riksdag to decide the policy of public assistance.

It goes without saying that there has been a good deal of controversy on this policy. Some people think that we have gone too far, that people are brought to rely too much on the help they may receive from the public, and that the state will not be able to bear its responsibilities if our economic position should be weakened. The Socialist party has of course been most zealous for developing socio-political legislation, while other parties have laid stress on the difficulties. It must be emphasized, however, that the foundations of this legislation were laid long before the Socialists had a commanding position in our political life and that no party has in principle been opposed to it. The controversies have been centered on the amount of help rather than on the fundamental question whether the state should help.

Important technical and administrative problems have been raised by the ramified and complicated socio-political legislation of recent times. How shall all the different forms of assistance be supervised? How can a rational connection between them be brought about? How can the administration avoid letting some citizens profit unjustly by several sorts of measures, while at the same time others are left without help? The problem of a rational coordination of the different branches of relief legislation is at this very moment a great political issue.

It still remains to say a few words about such forms of assistance as are not impressed by the general socio-political ideals of our days, for the state has in a number of other ways used its money to lighten the burdens of citizens. Subventions and loans have been given to several branches of industry. Real estate credit has to a very great extent been organized under the guarantee of the state. New lines have been tried in the agricultural crisis of the last decade.

A complicated system of agricultural adjustment has been built up. It is difficult to describe its methods in a few words. It may be enough to say that help has been given in many different forms to agriculturists who suffer from difficulties. Thus, for instance, the state has undertaken to purchase corn that cannot be sold at reasonable prices; this means a gigantic subvention to agriculture. In other cases help is given by direct subsidies to a production that is not profitable. This is, for instance, the meaning of the so-called milk regulation: subsidies are given to the export production of butter at the cost of the production of milk for home consumption. Loans and subventions are given in other forms also. The gist of this agricultural policy is that a sort of balance has been established. Before it was introduced, one might say the state had in a way favored the workers, especially in industry; now the farmers claim and receive their share in public support. This means, however, a complete revolution in the position and the minds of our agricultural class. They were always used to trust to their own forces; even in the days of increasing social interdependence they represented for a long time an individualistic element in society, a considerable moral force. Now they have been brought to rely more than before on public support. By a sudden change they have been made cogs in that mighty machinery of solidarity which the modern state forms. The "state farmer" is a slogan very often heard, and as a matter of fact it has some meaning. It seems as if the farmers will have to try a new kind of citizenship.

JUDICIAL REVIEW OF PUBLIC
ADMINISTRATION

THERE are, then, several sorts of material benefits the state bestows upon the citizens. But the very basis of state activity should not be forgotten; it is administering law and justice also. It may be said that in Sweden there is general confidence in the righteousness, the honesty, and the effectiveness of the judiciary and the execution of the law.

A foreigner will unquestionably be struck by some formalistic and bureaucratic methods used in our courts. The procedure is to a great extent in writing; before the higher courts the parties do not, as a rule, appear personally at all. Here there is clearly a need of reform, and reforms are now being prepared. It would seem then that up to now access to justice has been somewhat difficult, that it has not really a popular character. But there are other traits, too. The participation of laymen in the law courts has already been mentioned. Litigation is not very expensive, and it is possible to conduct a suit without the help of lawyers. Law is not to the same degree as in many other countries a secret science, accessible only to a narrow circle of the initiated. It is in principle embodied in statutes, not in precedents of the courts difficult to understand. So it has always been in Sweden. There is a firm tradition of law codification coming from the Middle Ages down to our own times. Codification means that it is easier for laymen to ascertain what rights and what duties they have. It means that law may live in the minds of laymen as well as of lawyers. A statute book, issued every year and containing all statutes in force except those that have only a very special bearing, will be found on the shelves of many Swedish laymen.

The judiciary falls, however, a little outside the scope of my survey, insofar as it has to do with civil and criminal cases. On the other hand it is of great importance to know in what ways citizens may guard their rights against mistakes and encroachments of state and municipal authorities.

In this connection I may first of all direct your attention to the peculiar rules on the publicity of public documents. Anyone who is dissatisfied with the way in which he has been treated by administrative authorities has access to the documents of the case. Here he may see what he is acting against, and the arguments raised to his disadvantage. He may discover that his case has aroused dissension and hesitation; perhaps he may find that some authority has held the opinion that he should have had what he asked for. The publicity of the documents is thus of a very great importance in strengthening the position of people who have claims against the public. This brings us to the question how the citizen should proceed if he thinks he has been injured in one way or another.

There is first the method of suing the officers personally before the general courts. In this way the citizen may have the pleasure of seeing them punished and the more material advantage of money damages, if the officer has the money to pay. It may also be of some value to have a controversial question of law settled by a court. I have already mentioned in another connection that most faults an officer may commit are subject to punishment. There is, however, the noteworthy difficulty that a private citizen cannot, as a rule, himself sue state officers. But he may apply to the solicitor general, who is elected every year by the riksdag to watch over courts and civil service, and who is especially charged to intervene when officers have committed grave faults and when administrative and judicial practice seems to imperil the general rights of the citizens. The solicitors general have nearly always been well qualified for their delicate task. Generally speaking if the citizen who asks for help has good grounds for his complaints, he will be helped in one way or another. The solicitor general may bring an action against the officer, or he may with his great authority convince him and persuade him to rectify his error, if that is possible.

Secondly, it is in some cases possible for the citizens to sue not only the officers but the state (the Crown) in the general courts. In this way the Crown may be compelled, for instance, to pay when the administrative authorities have refused to do so. This way is, however, practicable only in cases of contract and some similar situations. Is the citizen also entitled to sue the Crown in order to have an award for damages the administrative authorities have caused to him? This question, which is being discussed nowadays in all countries, is a problem in Swedish law too. There are a few statutory provisions securing a right of indemnity, but as a matter of fact the courts have gone further. In several cases they have found the Crown liable according to general legal principles.

On the whole, however, it may be said that the general courts do not play nearly the same role as in the Anglo-Saxon countries as safeguards against the encroachments of administration; I have mentioned earlier that they do not control legislation either. To be sure, we claim, as eagerly as in those countries, that the administration should act under a rule of law; but this does not mean that the same principles should always be valid for the relations between the Crown and the citizens as for the mutual relations of citizens, nor does it mean that the general courts should intervene in all cases. And there is not, and has not been, any demand for extending their powers to control administration.

Instead of that, the rights of the citizens are secured by another institution: the administrative appeal (*besvär*). It is a general principle of our administrative law that every decision of an administrative authority concerning the rights of a citizen may be complained of within a certain space of time; before that time has elapsed the decision is not, as a rule (there are of course many exceptions), valid and obligatory. The appeals are brought either before a superior administrative authority or before special authorities instituted for this purpose; we call them administrative courts.

All sorts of decisions made by state authorities are subject to this form of review. Just to mention a few examples —a citizen may appeal in questions about public elections, taxes, or customs; he may appeal if he does not get a permit or license he thinks he is entitled to, or if he has not been appointed to an office he has applied for. A municipality may appeal against a decision of the governor concerning its duties (for instance according to the highways statute, or the health regulations) or its rights (when a subvention has been refused, for example). The decisions of municipal authorities are also subject to appeal. If the municipal boards administering a certain branch of legislation act in such a way as to make citizens complain, the citizens have the same right of appeal as if the decision had been made by a state authority. Appeals may be made against an order from the Health Board to drain a building lot, against the

Buildings Board for not authorizing a new building, against the Poor-Law Board for refusing to give assistance, against the decisions of the Assessment Board, and so on. As soon as the application of a statute has been entrusted to the municipalities, they become subject to this control. Besides these municipal boards (administrative authorities, properly speaking), the municipal councils (i.e., the municipal representations) are also exposed to the intervention of state authorities after appeal. In this case we have the remarkable rule that anyone, whether legally interested in the case or not, is entitled to appeal. There is in this way a sort of *actio popularis* against illegal measures of the municipalities.

It has been mentioned that the control is exercised either by the superior administrative authorities or by special administrative courts. Among the administrative authorities that settle appeal questions are the governors (who, for instance, as a rule judge appeal cases brought in against the municipal councils and boards) and the central offices. Following the purely administrative line to its end, one arrives at the king in council, that is to say, the government. It may be said that one is not very effectively protected against encroachments of the administration by the administrative authorities themselves. This is true, but not so true as one would be inclined to suppose on theoretical grounds. The characteristic features of Swedish administration should not be forgotten. The administrative authorities have always been accustomed to look upon appeal cases as a sort of judicial work. It is a firm tradition that they should be handled from a legal point of view, in that spirit which prevails in the judiciary. And there are traits in the structure of the administrative offices that make them answer reasonably well to these demands: the independence of the civil servants, their unremovability, the publicity of documents, and so on. The legal education of civil servants is also important; generally one or more lawyers always have to take part in the treatment of an appeal case. For deciding appeal cases a central office is very often transformed to a board of three members, where the decision is taken by a majority vote. As a matter of fact the decisions made by administrative authorities in appeal cases are generally felt to correspond fairly well to the demand for justice. Municipal politicians, for instance, find it quite natural to be put under that control which is exercised by appeals to the governor.

But of course the administrative courts afford better guarantees for judging the cases according to legal rules and principles. Among these courts the so-called Court of Government (*regeringsrätten*) should be especially mentioned. It was instituted in 1909 to take over many appeal cases that were previously settled by the government. According to the principle that cases involving questions of law, roughly speaking, fall under the jurisdiction of this court, it now decides, as a court of final instance, nearly all the cases coming from the municipalities, questions on public elections, taxation, health legislation, building legislation, patent legislation, questions concerning public subsidies to municipalities and to private persons, and many others. As a matter of fact, only a few questions are left to the government, such as, for instance, questions of appointment. There are other administrative courts too: the Chamber Court (*kammarrätten*), which decides, among other questions, poor-law cases and complaints of civil servants who have not received the salary they think they are entitled to; the Court of Insurance (*försäkringsrådet*), which handles accident insurance legislation. In every province there is an Assessment Revision Board (*prövningsnämnd*), which also may be regarded as a court. It takes up appeals against the municipal assessment boards; its own decisions may be appealed against first in the Chamber Court and then in the Court of Government; tax questions may thus pass through four stages, while other cases seldom require more than two or three.

The administrative courts generally consist of lawyers. Some of the members of the Court of Government may however be civil servants without legal education. In the Court of Insurance there are some members who represent employers' and workers' organizations, and the assessment revision boards consist mainly of laymen.

When an appeal case is brought before an administrative authority or an administrative court, the legality of the act complained of should in the first place be considered. This is the very meaning of an administrative judiciary. And in some cases, such as the decisions of municipal councils, this question of legality is the only one that may be considered. The Court of Government judges whether the municipality has acted in the forms prescribed by law and whether it has exceeded the authority it has according to law. But the court is not entitled to inquire whether, within these boundaries, the municipality has acted reasonably, or wisely, or if it has taken care of its own interests, and so on. In this way the principle of municipal independence is maintained. In other cases, however, there are no restrictions as to the points of view that may be applied and the questions that may be raised in an appeal case. In French and German administrative law there is the well established rule that a court cannot nullify an act because, according to its opinion, *le pouvoir discrétionnaire, das freie Ermessen* should have been used in another way. In American law there are also boundaries of a similar sort that the courts do not exceed. But in Sweden the authority that judges an appeal case, whether it be an administrative authority or an administrative court, has exactly the same powers as the authority against whose decision the appeal is made. If it thinks the decision appealed is unwise, from practical, social, or economic points of view, it may nullify it. And not only nullify it; it may also reform the act, i.e., put another decision in the place of the decision disapproved of. The decisions of municipal boards are also subject to criticism and reformation in this way. The Chamber Court may intervene if it thinks that a poor-law board should have given pecuniary assistance to a person instead of sending him to a poorhouse. The Court of Government investigates whether the measures taken by the Health Board are impractical, and so on.

It may seem somewhat strange that courts meddle in this way with questions of administrative efficiency. You must remember, however, that the courts are administrative courts, with special competence for handling administrative questions. And of course they are rather cautious in opposing the decisions of authorities that know more about facts and practical issues than they do. As a matter of fact it is not usual to have the decisions in appeal cases criticized as fettering unduly the discretionary activity of administration. On the other hand, the power of the courts, discreetly used as it is in most cases, is thought to be of great value. It is particularly important as maintaining legal points of view in that obscure twilight zone where in other countries a great uncertainty as to the reach of the powers of the courts generally prevails, because it is difficult to say whether you have to do with execution of law or administrative discretion, with questions of law or questions of fact. The courts are thus enjoining upon administration the fundamental principle that public power, especially when it touches the interests and the rights of citizens, should not be exercised arbitrarily, and that in the realm of discretion as well as in application of the law the administration should act with consistency and righteousness. They are maintaining within the administration that combination of legal and practical points of view which we have always thought to be of great value as a safeguard of the rights of citizens.

It is unnecessary to describe the procedure by which appeal cases are treated. It may be enough to say that it is very simple, before the courts as well as before administrative authorities. It is simple and it is above all very cheap. There is no good reason why a citizen who believes he has been wronged should hesitate to maintain his rights by an appeal. The Court of Government alone judges some thousands of cases every year. Thus the intervention of the courts is not brought about only in extraordinary cases, or haphazardly. It does not have the character of an extraneous, incalculable force, disturbing the ordinary work of administration.

This observation may also be elucidated from another point of view. If I have not misunderstood American law, the possibility of intervention of the courts against administrative decisions, as well as against statutes, means that the validity of such acts is usually questionable. It may happen that long after a decision is made or a statute promulgated the courts may declare it null and void. From the Swedish point of view this would seem an intolerable uncertainty. In the interest of public security we want it decided in advance whether an act of a public authority is valid or not. Well, an administrative act concerning the rights of a citizen is not valid before the term for making an appeal has elapsed; and if an appeal is made, the validity is suspended until the competent authority has approved of it. But after that time has elapsed—or after the decision has been approved by that authority which acts as the last instance—the validity of the act cannot any more be questioned: it is final and obligatory. The scrutiny made in the appeal case may thus be described not as a control from without but as an integrating part of administration itself, to make it work steadily according to law and legal principles and to give it such an indisputable authority that the citizens can feel safe in their relations with the government.